NK
4893
.C48
cy.1

Chisman, Evelyn

Small dolls & other
collectibles

SMALL DOLLS

&

Other Collectibles

Evelyn Meade Chisman

DRAKE PUBLISHERS INC. NEW YORK·LONDON

Cop. 1

Special thanks to all of the wonderful people who were willing to share their dolls and their knowledge with me. To my friend, Norma Quinn, for all the happy hours we have had doll hunting, but especially for the 14-hour Saturday we spent gathering material for the book at a doll and antique show. To my editor, Elliot Roberts, for all of his good and patient advice; to Lee Kanstrup of the Dark Room Lab who helped me, for endless hours, to prepare the pictures for the book; to Roger Fremier for his professional touch on some of the pictures: I extend my most humble thanks to all of you.

Evelyn Meade Chisman

To my parents, Russell L. and Bonnie V. Meade who, even during the Great Depression, always managed to place a beautiful doll under the Christmas tree for my sister, Lois, and me; and to my son, Gregory Steven Chisman, the real doll in my life.

Published in 1978 by
Drake Publishers, Inc.
801 Second Avenue
New York, N.Y. 10017

Small Dolls and Other Collectibles
LC: 77-15903

ISBN: 0-8473-1665-3

Book Design: Harold Franklin

Printed in the United States of America

contents

INTRODUCTION

Although beautiful old dolls from earliest times
can be seen in museums throughout the world,
this book brings to you a sampling of dolls you
can find today and add to your collection. It
will touch on only a few of the many thousands
of small dolls that are still waiting to be collected.
You will find dolls ranging from the primitive to the sophisticated, from the humble to the
extravagant. They all have a place in our history.
For dolls are, in reality, a mirror of ourselves.

Evelyn Meade Chisman

Much of this book is a guide to flea markets, garage sales, doll and antique shows, rummage sales, junk shops—anyplace and everyplace dolls are apt to be found. It traces the steps of bargain hunters caught up in the fascinating hobby of doll collecting.

Beautiful dolls are waiting everywhere to be found. For the would-be collector who hesitates to start collecting dolls because of the expense, take heart. The price you may see on an old doll is not necessarily the price you will have to pay for it. Part of the fun of searching for old dolls is to find them at bargain prices. On some occasions you will pay the full listed price for a doll you can't do without, but this can be averaged out by obtaining other dolls for your collection at a fraction of their real value. Although doll prices have soared in the past few years, there is still time to start a good collection and at the same time develop a "nest egg" in the form of a valuable collection. Dolls are an excellent investment for the small investor. All predictions agree— doll values are on the rise.

This chapter is devoted to identifying places where dolls can be found today. You may find others, still undiscovered in your travels, although there are few places collectors have not been, including overseas.

Where to Find Doll Bargains

Flea Markets—Indoor and Outdoor

If you have not been to the flea markets, you may be missing some prize doll finds. Flea markets are flourishing in the United States and they can be a refreshing oasis for both widely travelled and beginning doll collectors.

Outdoor flea markets are held mostly on the weekends, in drive-in theaters, fairgrounds, or anyplace where a large number of people can gather to set up tables with bargains for sale. By word-of-mouth, the excitement of this weekend bargaining arena has grown and it is quite certain that no matter where you live, there is a flea market close by.

Even collectors who hold out for dolls in excellent condition can find dolls meeting their expectations here. It may be necessary to look over many tables of dishes, tools, Creeping Charlies, and old bottles, but persistence will win out for the dolls are there—if not one week, then possibly the next.

Dolls on exhibit, Monterey Presidio, September, 1977.
Courtesy of Doris Quinn

Sign at outside flea market antique show in San Juan Bautista, California, August, 1977.

Some flea markets are better than others. Large outdoor flea markets tend to become commercial, with permanent booths set up for year-round use, filled with never-before-used articles such as pottery, wigs, clothing, and hanging baskets. In this case, check the outside areas around the commercially centered booths. This is where the non-commercial flea market sellers will set up their tables. If you see no dolls, begin asking for them. The word will spread and sellers may bring dolls the next time. Do not be afraid to ask questions or to start a conversation with some of the sellers. Important doll information has been passed from one collector to another over a flea market table. Often a seller may have older, more valuable dolls that were not put out on the table for the general public to handle; take a chance and ask.

Dolls are being sold at outdoor flea markets at 20—50 percent below the original price shown in doll books, especially if they need to be cleaned and dressed. Flea market sellers are usually bargain hunters themselves and do not have large investments in their dolls. Do not be too shy to bargain on a price. It is great fun and you will be surprised how many real bargains you can get this way. If the seller will not bargain and you do not feel happy páying the price asked, don't get it. There will always be another chance to find a good bargain. Buying a doll should be a happy and exciting experience; getting the doll for a bargain price is half the fun.

Indoor flea markets consist of many small open shops housed under one roof. It is certainly worthwhile to check these areas, since usually at least one or two feature some dolls. Prices are fairly reasonable and local customers are usually able to purchase dolls on repeat visits for less than the shopper who is just passing through. You will find that the friendships you make while pursuing your doll-collecting hobby become a valuable part of the overall enjoyment you receive.

Inside and Outside Antique Shows
Seeing the popularity of outdoor flea markets, antique dealers are beginning to move their shows outside, too. Long tables are set in a parklike area, usually during the mid-summer months. There are happy exchanges of dollars for treasures, while the

smell of barbecued chicken and fresh-popped corn pervades the air. It is a festive occasion with licensed sellers bringing their merchandise from a hundred mile radius to these outdoor sales. Here you may pay the top price for a doll, but you will find antique dolls in very fine condition. For example, at such a show this writer found a rare eleven-inch Shirley Temple composition doll of the 1930s in mint condition down to the printed ribbon on the dress.

Inside antique shows are held several times a year by various groups of antique dealers and at least a few old dolls are always included. Admission of $1.50–$3.00 is charged to these inside showrooms, but the knowledge a collector will gain by viewing all the antiques is well worth the price.

Garage Sales

If you frequently visit garage sales, you will find dolls that you want sooner or later. However, sometimes only household goods are sold at a garage sale. In other words, you may have to search through many garage sales before you find any dolls. But once you do find one with dolls, there is usually a chance to get a real bargain. This is where many flea market sellers buy their dolls for resale. It would be safe to say that a doll bought at a garage sale for 50 cents could ordinarily be sold for $3 at a flea market.

Antique store in New Monterey, California.

You will find more modern dolls at garage sales. Considering the good investment dolls have been to date, it is wise to buy inexpensive modern dolls in good condition if they are at bargain prices. You may have the chance to sell or trade them for older dolls later.

Entire collections have been found at garage sales, such as a series of Nancy Ann Storybook dolls or a set of dolls from foreign lands. Often you can purchase a whole collection for a small price. Garage sale dolls are usually clean and well-preserved, since they have not had to travel about to arrive at the selling table. You can also try bargaining at garage sales, although some inexperienced sellers may look shocked at such a suggestion. Nevertheless, it's worth a try.

Arrive early, don't dawdle too long, and get on to the next sale. Your greatest competitors are dealers looking for bargains to add to their inventories. Plot your course the night before by checking the newspaper ads and organizing the addresses to make your driving route as short as possible. Note the opening times and arrive a little early. The first morning of a sale, from 8 A.M. to 11 A.M. is usually prime bargain time, although the sale may extend three or more days. Also, re-check the sale just before closing time because some householders discount drastically just to get rid of excess goods.

Rummage Sales
Although rummage sales are not the best places to find dolls, do not discount them completely. If you can arrive early and the merchandise has not been purchased before the doors are open to the public, a quick check of the toy and antique tables may be worthwhile. Pin cushion dolls and figurines are more likely to be found at rummage sales than play dolls.

Doll Shops
Flea market and garage sale buffs usually like other collectibles and memorabilia as well as dolls; thus the time spent searching these areas for doll bargains can be rewarding although no dolls are found. However, if a doll collector is not interested in other items, doll shops are good places to search. Doll shops, unlike antique stores, carry dolls of all ages (although more and more modern dolls are popping up in antique stores).

Visiting doll shops can also keep you up to date on the current value of your own collection. Quite often the doll shops carry dolls in their original ensembles, making them more desirable and valuable. If you already have the same doll without the clothing, you can learn how your own doll should be dressed. Doll clothes, patterns, and books relating to doll clothes are also in these shops. Selecting a doll shop with a friendly, patient owner is discussed in Chapter 2.

Doll Clubs and Doll Shows
Doll clubs have unlimited information on dolls. Members often trade or sell dolls to each other. At club meetings, members happily gather to catch up on all the doll news. Doll-club members enjoy cer-

tain advantages, such as a group rate for doll publications, discounts on doll-book purchases, and full information on coming doll show events.

Attending a doll show is not only a fantastic experience in doll appreciation, but also a wonderful way to get to meet other collectors. Most doll collectors have researched their dolls well and are happy and willing to share their knowledge with each other. At a selling show all the dolls are for sale. An exhibit is for viewing only. A show may be a combination of both. In the exhibition shows, ribbons are given for the best exhibits. Doll publications such as *Doll News* will keep the collector fully informed of the large shows and winners throughout the United States.

Many doll clubs exhibit their dolls for charity purposes. Dolls can play an important part in any kind of pageant celebrating our past. In Pacific

A well-stocked table with bisque, hard plastic, vinyl, and stuffed dolls. Moss Landing, California, outside flea market and antique show, July, 1977. *Courtesy of Maison de Poupées, Fresno, California*

Grove, California, one of the annual celebrations in 1974 included many nostalgic replays of yesterday. In one of the exhibition halls, members of the community brought their old dolls to be viewed by the general public. Doll shop owners and collectors alike shared their treasures. In this hall a fashion show was given, with women of the town wearing authentic old gowns. Forming a backdrop, as the ladies paraded and twirled in their lovely dated ensembles, were exhibits of beautiful old dolls. It was a typical American scene—recapturing the past with realistic flamboyancy, laughing, and sharing, and learning together.

The early European bisque and china dolls are very highly prized in the doll collecting world. They number among the most beautiful, the oldest, and the rarest dolls still to be found.

When the process of manufacturing these coveted dolls first began is unknown. The majority of the dolls preserved before the mid 1800s seem to be the smaller china ones, but the bisques were soon to follow. By 1860 records clearly show that the doll manufacturing business had a firm foothold in Europe and soon dolls were being produced by the thousands daily.

Doll collectors will find that most of these bisque and china dolls dating from 1860—1925 are now in the hands of collectors. Those still for sale are found in quantity only in doll shops, with the bisque far outnumbering the china dolls. Prices are escalating and the number of dolls of this era are becoming harder to find each year. A collector will soon find that the majority of old bisque and china dolls are selling for one hundred to five hundred dollars, with some rare dolls selling for thousands of dollars. This poses a problem for collectors who must have other demands on their budget. However, this is not an insurmountable problem and later we shall discuss ways to acquire fine old dolls.

Many collectors have started very simply. Perhaps an old remembered doll was rediscovered in an old chest, or a garage sale doll purchased for one dollar sparked an old interest that had lain dormant since the last doll was tucked away by a growing young woman. But a simple beginning does not guarantee anything in the game of doll collecting! The more knowledge the collector gains about old dolls, the deeper the interest becomes and the more worldly the wants become. Sooner or later the collector will come to the old bisque and china dolls. They must surely be part of a growing doll collection.

In becoming acquainted with bisque and china dolls, you need to find a doll shop with a patient and understanding owner—one who will answer questions and allow you to examine some of the old dolls *at your leisure*. There is much to learn about old dolls. Rushing through a doll shop simply will not do, and gazing through a glass counter at untouchable dolls is worthless. Most doll shop owners,

chapter 2

Porcelain-Type Bisque and China Dolls

11" china doll with molded blonde hair, painted blue boots, painted features, stuffed body. *Courtesy of Joe Cleary*

4½" china doll with painted features, cloth-stuffed body, china legs, painted shoes, no marks; cost $20. *Courtesy of Laura Ham, Circle H shop, Soquel, Calif.*

China head, arms, and legs; stuffed body. *Courtesy of Laura Ham*

once they are convinced that a person is a serious collector, will trust them to handle the dolls carefully. The dolls must be felt, turned over, searched for identifying marks, examined closely and at arms length, and studied carefully from top to bottom: from the outside clothing to the daintiest undergarments.

The difference between bisque and china will soon become apparent. Bisque is not glazed. Bisque dolls therefore do not have the glass-tone, shiny effect that characterizes china dolls. You will probably prefer one or the other. Whatever the preference, each collector should have some knowledge of how both these types of dolls were manufactured.

The quality of the pure white clay used for early European china and bisque dolls has been referred to as porcelain. It was, in other words, a clay of high quality, finely ground to produce dolls of exceptionally smooth texture. Most bisque and china dolls do not have the shell—like translucency and light weight normally expected in fine pieces of porcelain. They do, however, contain kaolin, a pure white paste extracted from an earthen clay mixture through a process of soaking, filtering and straining. The French term *kaolin* originated from the Chinese word *kao-ling*, a high mountain peak, and from such mountains in the province of Kiangsi, China, came the first exports of fine white clay to be received in Europe.

CHINA

It is conjectured that china dolls were manufactured in backyard kilns in Europe before the onset of the Industrial Revolution. Unfortunately, many of these china dolls are unmarked. Germany manufactured most of the early china doll heads. They were often molded by hand or pressed into molds; the firing of these heads often took several days. Then they were dipped in a glaze and fired a second time. China dolls derived from "hard paste" have proved to be the most valuable, since the hardness of the clay allowed delicate detailing and more perfected proportions. The "soft paste" china dolls have not withstood so graciously the passing of the years. Most of the old china dolls have molded hair and the heads extend down to include the shoulders.

Three china dolls, 6½", 9½", 6½". All
have studded bodies, bisque arms and
legs. *Courtesy of Merrill Maudlin*

Sew holes were left on either side of the front and
back of the shoulderplate to allow for attachment to
the body.

Parian and pink lustre china dolls are very
highly prized and quite rare. The parian dolls,
although glazed, were not covered with a complexion coloring. With the usual blonde hair and
marblelike appearance, they are out of the ordinary
and very collectible. Pink lustre heads were
produced by the addition of pink oxide to the clay,
resulting in a doll with pastel pink complexion
coloring. This has made them much sought after by
collectors. (Parian: Germany 1850-1870)

Identifying Old China Dolls
Besides the shroud of mystery surrounding the
beginnings of china dolls, there is disagreement
among experts as to their evolution. However, certain characteristics of old china dolls have been discovered to distinguish them from later models.
Although each collector faces the risk of misidenti-

7" china doll representing Amy of *Little
Women*. Painted features, all china except
stuffed body, all original with pencil tied
to right hand, gold painted shoes. From
1940s garage sale, $5.

Bisque doll shown with box in which author found doll head at flea market for $5. Doll is pictured after doll hospital mended chipped shoulder, added wig and body. Manufactured by Armand Marseilles. Head marked "Mabel."

A famous 7" googly-eyed, Armand Marseilles,1920s bisque-headed doll. Marks: 323/A 11/0 N. Shoes made by owner's father. *Courtesy of Mary Williams*

fication of these unmarked dolls, the following is a general guide:

Finish: A "pit" or dark unfinished spot on a china doll is a good indication that the doll is old. Imperfection blemishes on the surface are due to poor firing methods or dust/dirt clinging to the clay during firing. As the process was improved and refined, these blemishes disappeared. Wear marks on the back of the doll's head from a child lying it down is another clue of antiquity.

Coloring: Old china doll heads had a delicate orangish red tint to the lips and small dots of this color were painted on the nostrils and the inside corners of the eyes. A slight line of the same color was also painted above the eye to indicate the eyelid. Eyebrows were delicate and unpretentious. Cheeks were faintly painted in pink tones (although there are some "apple-cheeked" old china dolls with high, round coloring on the cheeks). The flesh coloring on old china heads was often uneven and this coloring in some cases only extended to the neck.

Styles: The molded heads of china dolls reflected hairstyles of the early 1800s which could be a center part, with the hair pulled tightly down, and curls near the ears; or the hair combed severely back from the forehead and up from the nape of the neck to an accented topknot on the crown. Blonde china dolls with bangs did not come into vogue until the latter part of the nineteenth century. Black hair and blue eyes were the most popular colors. Glass eyes in a china doll are rare. Prior to 1860, the shoes of old china dolls were flat-soled, often fashioned into a boot. The heads had much deeper shoulders than the later models.

Unfortunately, many of the tiny china dolls lack the detail that larger chinas have, which makes it even more difficult to distinguish age.

BISQUE

The majority of the fine bisque dolls from 1860-1920s were manufactured in Germany and France, although other countries such as England and Italy also had their master craftsmen, but did not export their products on such a large scale.

Because the bisque dolls can still be found in greater quantity than the china dolls (or the earlier papier mâché, wax, and wood dolls), these are the dolls that most collectors trade *up* for. An early bisque doll purchased today instantly adds a greater value to a collection because of its near-antiquity. Although many collectors may gather dolls for their own personal enjoyment, it seems reasonable, with all the energy expended searching and trading for dolls, that a serious collector should expect ultimately to own a valuable collection—a "nest egg" for the future, or "something to pass down to future generations." Doll collecting can, in other words, be a combination of a delightful hobby and a profitable business venture.

The German Influence

Germany was the leading manufacturer of bisque dolls. The making of dolls was often a family profession. Backyard kilns were a familiar sight in small German villages by the mid 1850s. Who would have dreamed that these dolls with so humble a beginning would become cherished possessions of doll collectors the world over in the next hundred years? Many of these family dollmakers produced only the doll heads. As the popularity of the dolls grew, doll factories began to appear.

Large deposits of white clay were found in many areas of Germany. As it was processed, the clay, of doughlike consistency, was kneaded, rolled, and pressed into plaster molds. The molded head-pieces were fired in a very hot oven to dry and harden the clay. After this greenware was sanded to a smooth finish and holes cut for the eyes and mouth, overall coloring was applied. The detailing of facial features demanded the expertise of patient artists. A doll's origin can often be identified by the fine feather brush strokes of the eyebrows, or the cherub-painting of the lips. The bisque was fired a second time after the coloring. Then eyes were inserted and set with cement or wax held securely by plaster. The crown of the bisque heads to be exported were cut out to make them lighter, since even in those days manufacturers had to be concerned with assessments on exported goods (the doll heads were taxed according to weight). Wigs would cover the cutout areas. Upon completion, heads were crated and shipped on to other dollmakers or factories, where bodies and limbs were added to complete the doll.

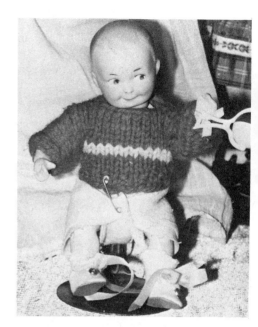

Armand Marseilles' "Googly" pictured at doll show in Vallejo, California, November 1977. Composition body, price: $325.
Courtesy of Betty Musser

8½" Armand Marseilles with painted bisque head, composition body and limbs. Scottish kilt, tam and jacket. Priced $25-$45 at flea market.
Courtesy of Norma Quinn

10" Armand Marseilles bisque-headed Indian, papier-mâché body. Pictured at Vallejo doll show, November, 1977, $99.00. *Courtesy of Betty Musser*

Three bisque doll heads from 1894. 3" Armand Marseilles, marked 5/0 DEP/ Made in Germany; the smallest, 1904, Edwarda Juan, Made in Austria. *Courtesy of Merrill Maudlin*

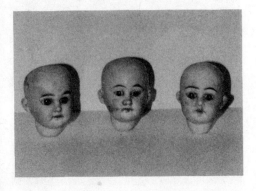

Fortunately, the doll collector with limited resources may have a good chance to attain bisques, since many of them are within the realm of the average budget. Small dolls by German dollmaker Armand Marseille are still relatively inexpensive. Marseille was a popular German dollmaker of the 1860s. His dolls were moderately priced at the time of manufacture, possibly because of inexpensive bodies, but the heads are certainly to be admired.

A Marseille doll head marked *Mabel/Germany* was found by this collector early one Sunday morning at an outdoor flea market in 1977. The doll head had been placed in a small box topped with clear plastic, marked *OLD DOLL HEAD-$5.00*. Only a small piece of the shoulder was chipped; otherwise the head, down to the tiny teeth, was in perfect condition. Where had the doll been found? In a Nevada dump! The woman selling the doll head was not especially interested in dolls, although she and her husband enjoyed searching for old artifacts. She had begun to restore the doll—had gone to a doll hospital and purchased eyes and some pieces of blonde mohair for a wig. Then, losing interest, she tucked the doll away for several years. This particular Sunday she decided to bring it to the flea market. What a thrill for a collector! Not only was it a beautiful old head, but available at a bargain price. The woman made a statement which I have heard many times after a pleasant doll transaction had been made: "I'm glad someone got it that will appreciate it." A doll hospital repaired the shoulder, added an authentic old leather body, and a dark brown wig (to match the eyebrows). For an expenditure of forty dollars, a fine bisque doll has taken a favorite spot in my collection.

Ernst Heubach was another popular dollmaker in Germany. He and Marseille were brothers-in-law, and for a time, around 1865, operated a doll factory (Koppelsdorfer Porzellanfabrik) in Koppelsdorf, Germany. Heubach's dolls were artfully modeled and fortunately many have come down to collectors in beautifully preserved condition. The bisque Heubach doll in illustration was purchased at an outside flea market recently for twenty-five dollars, a bargain price for such an old and beautiful doll. At the time she was purchased, it was a warm sunny day and the collector selling the doll had placed her facedown on the table to protect the wax in the eyes. Once the doll was turned over and the charm of her plump cheeks and black pupilless eyes were seen, it was impossible to leave without her!

There are many well known German doll companies and the collector will only become acquainted with the particular beauty of each manufacturer's product by seeing and examining the dolls herself. Kestner Doll Company is one of the most famous and respected German doll manufacturers. The company, founded in the 1840s, grew to employ several hundred people. Kestner is known to have used slip casting (the pouring of a thick liquid porcelain into the molds) and gave some of his early dolls fur eyebrows. However, the more prevalent heavy brushstroke brows are a distinguishing mark of a Kestner doll.

Simon and Halbig, another German doll company, was manufacturing small seven-inch dolls in 1899, along with much larger ones. Limited space prohibits discussing all the fine German doll makers, but there were many, and Germany will be forever known for the fine skill of her toymakers.

8½" Heubach-Koppelsdorf doll. Bisque head, brown pupilless sleep eyes, papiermâché body, human hair wig. Circa 1900. Value: $80-$120.
Photo by Roger Fremier

French Influence

Jumeau and Bru were the two leading French doll makers. France began by importing doll heads from Germany, but by 1862, M. Jumeau had perfected his own doll heads, using the talents of master artists to sculpt designs of awesome beauty. Jumeaus—some long-faced, all with mesmerizing large eyes—have gained fame not only because of the artistry of the dolls, but from the exquisite and elaborate costuming, typical of French fashioners.

French Bru dolls, darker complexioned beauties, are elegant. These *bebes incassables* ("unbreakable babies") were of course breakable up to a point, although the hardness of the clay and the excellent firing methods helped to make them more secure than thinner porcelains in the arms of a young child. The Bru factory, located near Paris, employed accomplished dressmakers and the singularly fashioned dolls won acclaim the world over.

French dolls are among the most coveted and sell for the highest prices. Nevertheless, a medium-sized Jumeau doll in excellent condition down to the shoes, marked "Jumeau" was recently seen in an an-

10" Kestner bisque baby marked 3 - 2/0. Composition body, blue sleep eyes, dimples in cheeks and chin, painted light brown hair and lashes, two baby teeth painted in upper mouth, 1917.
Courtesy of Ellen Souten

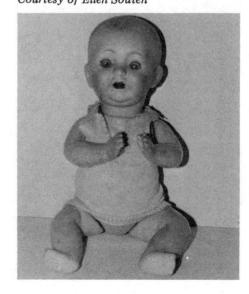

Part of doll display by Doris Quinn at Presidio of Monterey. (Front row, left to right) Kestner character bisque, sugar bisque from 1920s-30s, Kestner bisque with composition body, reproduction bisque. (Back row) Chase dolls with molded cloth heads, painted with oils. *Courtesy of Doris Quinn*

Small unmarked bisque doll seen at annual San Juan Bautista outside flea market & antique show, $125. *Courtesy the Coach Shop, Santa Cruz, California.*

tique show for only $15. On the other hand, without batting an eyelash, a collector purchased a French doll with pewter hands at a recent doll show for $1,000. But don't rush out to buy an air ticket for France, since collectors and dealers both state that dolls are very expensive there also.

It will take some fancy trading and bargaining if French dolls are your goal, but it can be accomplished.

American Influence

Two Americans made their mark in the doll world near the end of the bisque manufacturing boom. They were Pennsylvania-born Rose O'Neill with her famous Kewpie dolls and American sculptor-artist Grace Story Putnam creator of the still popular Bye-Low baby. More imitations of these two dolls have been made over the last fifty years than any of us could imagine.

Rose O'Neill's Kewpies made their debut as delightful drawings to accompany her poems, and perhaps their publication in the *Ladies Home Journal* of 1909 ignited the entire series of events that led these fat-tummied little creatures down the path of fame. Often linked with love and happiness, the Kewpie doll has become a part of our American heritage. Whatever the reason, the Kewpie dolls have been loved since they first became available as adorable bisque dolls in the early 1920s. The original Kewpies have O'Neill incised on the sole of the feet and a red and gold heart-shaped label glued on the chest. Marked on the back was a round label *Copyright, Rose O'Neill*. Even today there are replicas of these Kewpies being made. Kewpies have appeared as paintings, paper dolls, figurines, frozen dolls, hinged dolls, buttons, good luck charms, etc. The dolls have been made of bisque, celluloid, composition, cloth, rubber, metal and plastic—but the bisque will always be the best loved.

The Bye-Low baby is also still being duplicated today, even as bisques, although the factory-produced bisques do not have nearly the charm of the original Bye-Lows. As a sculptor, Grace Story Putnam was able to model a three-day-old baby's head, first in clay, then plaster, and then in life-size wax. Her famous search for a real life baby model ended in a Salvation Army nursery. By 1923, Bye-

Lows were on the market, being manufactured by Kestner. The first Bye-Lows were all-bisque, but soon composition and cloth bodies were substituted for economical reasons. *Grace S. Putnam* was incised on the head and the name was also stamped on the cloth body.

George Borgfeldt Company, a New York agent, helped some of the famous doll companies such as Kestner and Marseille distribute their dolls in the United States. Borgfeldt was involved both with the Kewpies and the Bye-Lows. Through Borgfeldt, arrangements were made for Kestner to manufacture the bisque Kewpies, with the approval of Rose O'Neill, and the association that began in 1912 lasted until World War I.

Identifying Old Dolls

It is wise to invest in a book listing all the doll markings. There are many reproductions of the old bisques coming onto the market. Although many of them are inferior to the texture and styling of the

Three bisques. (Left) 6½" all-bisque Kewpie. Marks: O'Neill on bottom of feet; $40 in antique store. (Center) 5½" bisque-head doll with composition body, golden blonde mohair wig, original provincial costume, from late 19th century. Mark: 211 (believed to be Kestner). (Right) 7" bisque doll believed to be French (Rabery and Delphieu). Composition body, brown sleep eyes, open mouth with four teeth, mohair wig. Marked 1909 DEP R 5/10 D. *Courtesy of Norma Quinn*

Rare 9" Maria marked K ★ R 101.
Bisque head, composition body, $950.
Courtesy of Betty Musser

14" Bru with leather kid body, wood arms
and legs, brown eyes, original clothes.
From collection of Mrs. Joseph Cleary.
*Courtesy of Joseph Cleary, Orinda Arts,
Orinda, California*

authentic old dolls and are easy to spot as reproductions, there are some very well done bisques that are also expensive. This does not mean these dolls are not worth collecting, but they should be identified as reproductions or new productions. Although it is the obligation of the seller to inform the purchaser of the age and identification of a doll, misinformation can innocently be passed from one person to another. Having a book available to check the markings is an extra precaution every doll collector should take before making a large investment in an old doll.

Following is a general guide meant to help the new collector identify old bisque dolls. It is not foolproof, since some inexpensive doll heads with more primitive bodies may be taken as older dolls, and the many variations of style and material make it impossible to completely categorize dolls according to age. However, certain characteristics can be kept in mind:

Old Bisque Dolls
(There was a combination used through all the years on dolls, such as different materials which were being experimented with—wood with kid, wood with composition, composition with bisque, etc.)

Bodies

1840s Jointed kid bodies stuffed with sawdust (tiny waistlines and plump hips on French dolls); wood bodies; cloth bodies stuffed with hay

1850 Gusset joints on kid bodies

Prior 1851 Adult dolls; child dolls added after 1851

1860 Cotton bodies w/leather arms on cheaper Jumeau dolls; early Jumeau dolls—jointed wood bodies covered with kid

After 1860 Machine sewn doll bodies (sewing machine invented 1846, but not widely used until 1860s)

1870 to 1880 Composition bodies, some ball-jointed; Jumeau dolls were unmarked until composition was used in 1880, then marked on body

Small bisque "Dream Baby" and larger bisque "Bye-Lo" baby, both designed by Grace Story Putnam.
Courtesy of Susan Hoy

After 1880 Extensive use of strung composition or wood for bodies (German dolls w/swivel necks)

1890 Rivet joints on kid bodies

1908 & 1909 Marseille doll bodies of pink canvas, stuffed legs and bisque lower arms

1911 Marseille wooden bodies and limbs, composition blow knee

Heads

Prior to 1860 Flirting eyes and pierced ears; used commonly after 1860

1860 Shoulder plate heads

1869 Swivel neck invented by Jumeau

Prior to 1870 Painted eyes or movable eyes with strings attached to the outside of the doll to manipulate movement (said to have begun in England by 1825)

8½" bisque German bonnet head doll, early 1900s. Pictured at Orinda doll show. $125.00. *Courtesy of Rhoda Shoemaker*

Exceptionally fine bisque half-figure with all silk pink container for gloves, hankies, hose or other of milady's accessories. Hands beautifully detailed.
Courtesy of Merrill Maudlin

1870 to 1880 Some lambs wool wigs noted

After 1880 Open mouths with teeth

Prior to 1900 Pupilless eyes (a point of disagreement among experts)

By 1880 Mohair and human hair wigs

1891 Country of origin must be marked on doll by law

Early 1900s Celluloid eyes popular for a short time

chapter 3

Japanese Influence

When World War I temporarily cut off the import of dolls from Europe to the United States, Japan stepped in and tried to duplicate the German and French bisques and chinas. Of special interest to the small-doll collector are the all-bisque and china dolls from one to eight inches which were produced during this time. The majority of these small dolls were not comparable in craftsmanship to the European dolls. The opaque bisques were composed of a coarsely ground clay, which resulted in a slightly rough, granular texture. Thus they were dubbed "stone bisque", or even more commonly called "sugar" or "salt" bisque. In general the dolls had wired or strung arms and legs, painted eyes, and short curly molded hair. Ribbons, flowers, and headbands were often molded onto the hair. Many of these dolls came unclothed and children were content to play with them this way, or clothed with scraps from mother's sewing basket. Some of these small dolls wore painted bathing suits and other clothing, including socks and shoes. However, this paint was not always refired and in time either wore off or was scrubbed off by fastidious young playmothers.

These small china dolls also were inferior in texture—bumpy and heavy for their size, with the painted features often sloppily applied, with dribbles of paint permanently bonded under the glaze of the china. Both tiny play dolls and figurines were produced in the same fashion, and the lack of intricate detail especially of the facial features makes them easy for even the beginning collector to spot as a secondary product.

These small dolls flooded the United States market in the 1920s and 30s and the American children who were spending their pennies in the dime and dry goods stores during these two decades didn't care one iota about the good or poor quality of the bisque or china; they simply loved them as adorable little dolls that were there when they needed them.

The author recalls playing with two Japanese bisque dolls in the early 1930s, nestling them together in a large kitchen matchbox padded with a piece of soft folded flannel. On one end was a black

Secondary Bisque and China Dolls

3¾" sugar bisque Indian man and woman, found in old New York brownstone apartment in 1970s, evidently uncovered in new condition. Oilcloth clothing with tiny beads, yarn hair, painted eyes, rabbit fur on brave's headdress, strung arms and legs, 1920s. Purchased at inside flea market in 1977 for $8.00 pair, value: $16 pair.
Photo by Roger Fremier

4" sugar bisque from 1930s, dressed only
in diaper, painted features. Marked MADE
IN JAPAN. Flea market price: $3.50;
doll shops: $9-$12. The depression glass
sugar bowl shown is "tea room" in green.
Value: $5.00 without cover.
Photo by Roger Fremier

3½-inch baby and on the other a white sugar bisque
doll with molded hair and "Betty Boop" eyes. These
dolls in their portable bedstead went everywhere.
Tucked in a safe, deep snowsuit pocket, they slid
down snow-packed Iowa hills, lent moral support to
the serious business of building plump, coal-eyed
snowmen, slept contentedly on the porch swing, and
sneaked into Sunday School in a shiny patent
leather purse, keeping company only with a white
handkerchief, tied at one corner to securely hold
pennies for the offering.

Doll collectors, accustomed to the more delicately designed French and German bisques, re-
garded these dolls as culls; but other collectors who
were wise enough to gather them up while prices
were low are having the last laugh—for some of the
larger of these "inferior" dolls are now selling for
twenty dollars each. These dolls are highly collectible today, probably because they are becoming quite
old, but their popularity may also be attributed to
the fact that many collectors today recall playing
with these very dolls when they were children.

It is still possible to find quite a few bargains in
these types of dolls, although prices seem to be rising gradually but steadily. Since these small dolls
were produced in all colors—black, brown, white,
flesh-toned, etc.—the collector still has a good
chance of finding a variety of them. It is interesting
to note that several dolls from this era have been

seen at flea markets, the by-product of an excavation by old bottle enthusiasts who happened to unearth them while searching for other old treasures. The smaller dolls, from one to four inches, range in price from $2-$4 at flea markets, junk shops and some antique stores, but the price rises as the doll becomes larger. Japan's flagrant copies of the Kewpie dolls and the Bye-Low baby seem to still be quite plentiful and are eagerly accepted by doll collectors, whether inferior or not.

FROZEN CHARLOTTE DOLLS

Many of the small bisque and china dolls dating especially from 1910-1935 have a double identity. There were dolls of comparable size and style made both by the skilled hands of European dollmakers and by Japanese manufacturers who cared little about quality, but were obsessed with quantity at a low price. A doll collector must be acquainted with both types of bisque and china in order to be able to determine whether or not a doll, say from the 1930s, is priced according to the quality of the bisque rather than by the date of manufacture. A collector may find a small Kestner doll from the early 1900s priced at over a hundred dollars, while a doll of approximately the same size and style, but manufactured by Japan in the less aesthetic stone bisque, will sell for a fraction of that; a fine Dresden-type pincushion doll which could have been manufactured at approximately the same time as a secondary china pincushion top doll will certainly demand a much higher price.

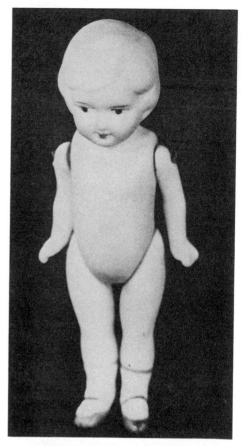

5¼" flesh-colored sugar bisque with wire arms and legs, painted brown shoes and blue-topped stockings, 1930s. Purchased from collector for $12.00. *Courtesy of Lois Harbert*

2½" sugar bisque, circa 1932, Frozen Charlotte type in molded one-piece body, painted features, straw skirt and orange paper lei. Straw hut 3-¾". Marks: MADE IN JAPAN. Found at church rummage sale with 10 cent price tag; $9 at doll shows. *Photo by Roger Fremier*

This confusion carries over into the dolls that have been named the Frozen Charlottes. Dolls called Frozen Charlotte range from the German china dolls of the early 1940s to the stone bisque dolls of the 1920s and 30s. Actually, the term *Frozen Charlotte* is simply a nickname for a certain type of stiff little doll, some with arms and legs close to the body (so they could easily be molded in one piece) and others with arms molded away from the body and legs apart.

The story of the Frozen Charlotte began after a blind singer, William Lorenzo Carter, heard a story and turned it into a ballad in 1833. The drama supposedly took place on New Year's Eve in Vermont.

As the story goes, "Fair Charlotte" was the only child of an adoring and indulgent father who prided himself in dressing his daughter in beautiful clothes. Charlie, a young suitor, appeared at Charlotte's door this fateful evening to take her to a New Year's Eve festivity. They were to ride fifteen miles to the village in Charlie's sleigh. Charlotte, vanity prevailing, elected to ride in style in a silken coat and shawl. Ignoring the pleadings of her mother to fold blankets around her, Charlotte cried,

(Left) 5" molded sugar bisque with red hat, strung arms and legs. Purchased from collector for $8.00. Marked JAPAN on back. (Right) Nippon version of "Little Bud," manufactured and patented in Germany in 1915. The fingers on left hand are raised in a "V" sign. Good quality bisque, "Baby Bud" across back, "Nippon" down side of shirt. Garage sale $1.00.

> Oh nay, oh nay,
> For to ride in the blankets muffled up
> I never can be seen.
> My silken coat is quite enough
> Besides, I have a silken scarf
> Which round my neck I'll throw.

As Charlie and Charlotte proceeded into the freezing night, five miles elapsed before Charlotte complained of being cold. After another five miles she was "growing warmer". When they reached the village, Charlie noticed she was like a monument.

> He tore the mantle from her brow
> On her face the cold stars shone.

When Charlie found Charlotte had frozen to death,

> his heart did break/And they both lie in one tomb.

And so from this sad tale was born the "Frozen

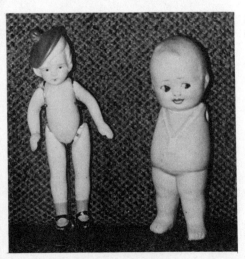

Charlotte" doll. Although there are slightly different versions of the ballad, the gist of the story is the same.

Pincushion Dolls

Pincushion dolls were extremely popular in the 1920s, and both Germany and Japan produced these dolls in fine and secondary china. Many of the doll torsos were quite dainty and posed like Dresden figures. From 1924-29, the flapper era influenced the modeling of these figures. Some pincushion dolls are posed with arms molded away from the body, a posture greatly preferred by some collectors. Skirts materials range from the loveliest of laces to plain cotton materials. Recently at a flea market a pincushion-type doll torso was seen tucked into the folds of a silken-type lamp shade—the type of bedroom lamp used as a reading light clamped onto the headboard.

Bonnet Dolls

A word should be mentioned here about bonnet dolls, for they too were made of both fine bisque and stone bisque. Some early fine-bisque bonnet dolls were produced in Germany from 1870-1900. Many of these dolls had real bonnets adorned with ribbons, flowers, and various trimmings. The later bonnet dolls had the hats molded onto their heads. This is the type of doll that is favored for reproduction. Since these dolls had all types of bodies, including jointed wood and kid, they were popular, out-of-the-ordinary dolls, and although children may have loved the baby dolls more, collectors are thrilled to have an authentic bonnet doll in their collection.

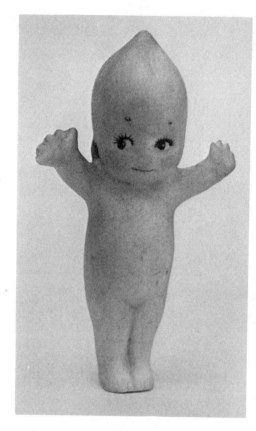

1¾" bisque Kewpie, blue wings, no marks. Garage sale price 10 cents, value $3.00.
Photo by Roger Fremier

Two pincushion dolls, from 1920-30s. (Foreground) Belonged to author in 1930s, made in Japan. (Background) Mounted on old wood thread holders. Flapper-type half-doll, marked Made in Germany. The price of pincushion dolls usually begins at $8 and, depending on age and quality, can go up to $50.

Author's 5" sugar bisque doll from 1934. Elastic strung arms, painted features, Kewpie-type hands. Marked MADE IN JAPAN on back. At flea markets and antique shows for $8-$12.

8" pincushion doll. Ceramic top marked OKC 1925. Painted features, dark mohair wig. *Courtesy of Lois Meade Harbert*

5" bisque with Shirley Temple-type curls, elastic strung arms and legs, painted shoes, hair painted gold, 1930s. Gift shop price $4.00, value $12.00.
Courtesy of Norma Quinn

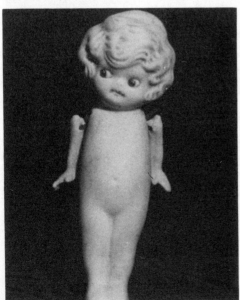

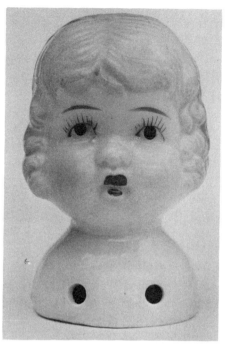

3" secondary china head, 1920s. Marks: Made in Japan stamped inside back shoulder. This head was attached to a silken, stuffed pin cushion with rectangularly shaped arms and legs. Purchased at garage sale for $2.00 by author's mother; value with body, in antique store, $10.00. *Photo by Roger Fremier*

Dutch pincushion doll with molded hat, holding molded cup and saucer. *Courtesy of Lois Meade Harbert*

Four sugar bisques, left to right: 2" Frozen-Charlotte type. 3" with painted hair and molded clothes, holding pink flowers, 1920s-30s. 1¼" bisque, probably used as cake decoration early turn of century. Painted 3" figure of boy, novelty from 1937 World's Fair, San Francisco, $3.

chapter 4

Wax and Papier-Mâché Dolls

It would be great fun to imagine that the very first wax-headed doll was simply made from a dollop of sealing wax. Gwen White, in her book *Antique Toys and Their Background*, describes a unique creation from the sixteenth century, which was not really a doll, but a pen wiper. A large fowl wishbone was used as the body, the legs being the two ends, which could be seen protruding from below the skirt like feet. The petticoats were of flannel and from this bit of cloth their practicality was confirmed—for the flannel was used to wipe the ink from the pens. Upon the tip of the bone sat the sealing wax—the only round and moldable substance that could be found for the head.

Nevertheless, was dolls had a much more serious role in doll history, no matter how delightful this thought might be. Early in history, the Chinese children played with wax shadow figures. In Italy, wax had been used for the making of crèche or crib figures since Bible times, and the churches held these small figures for special occasions. The bodies of these tiny figures were often made of linen, and the robes and gowns were of silk or velvet with elegant gold trim. Bavaria, Spain, England and Mexico also favored the medium of wax for religious crib figures, fashioning some from natural beeswax which contained some animal fat to make the wax more moldable. In the 1700s dolls were created with wax heads, and were stuffed with tow (flax or hemp fiber) and some even boasted "squeaker" voice boxes.

Wax museums, much like our modern ones, exhibiting life-size replicas of well-known persons, were quite popular in the 1800s, and it is suspected that once the process of modeling in wax was perfected, it was inevitable that small figures that could be used for dolls emerged from this artistic accomplishment. Wax was a good material for shaping the top part of the doll but it was not until later that arms and legs also were modeled in wax. When one considers that these dolls were quite sophisticated, with glass eyes—some weighted for opening and closing—complete with a waxed eyelid, some that contained a crier box, implanted hair, and pierced ears for earrings, it is rather wondrous that all of this could have been accomplished in what might be considered a less-than-hardy material.

In the early 1800s French, English and German doll artists were working in wax. Often only the head was wax, while the calico or muslin body was stuffed with such substances as cow hair, straw, or sawdust. At first only the wealthy could afford the wax dolls, which were dressed in fancy taffeta and silken gowns. In those days the hair was inserted through a rather long slit in the top of the head. This later created problems of crazing and long broken lines began to appear on some of the doll faces. It was learned that the painstaking process of inserting each hair individually with a hot needle worked better, but this made the dolls even more expensive.

In the 1851 London Exhibition, the stars of the exhibit were dolls modeled and clothed by Augusta Montanari, for which she was awarded a medal. Her wax dolls of varying ages were grouped into family gatherings and were accompanied by suitably scaled furniture. The Montanari dolls were ever after considered the aristocrats of wax dolldom. Not only were the dolls' hairs inserted individually, but eyelashes and eyebrows were fashioned in the same way. The eyes of her dolls were deep violet, blue, and gray. At the same exhibit, her husband, Napoleon Montanari showed sculptured life-sized models of Mexican Indians. The talent of the family was passed on to their son, Richard, who joined his mother in creating wax dolls (never in mass production). In spite of Augusta Montanari's death in 1846, Richard continued in the doll business over

Papier-mâché doll with molded hair, wood arms and legs, stuffed body, approximately 9", circa 1850. *Courtesy of Joe Cleary*

Two wax dolls of early origin. (Left) Brown glass eyes, kid arms, stuffed body, doll show price, $250. (Right) Blue glass eyes, papier-mâché limbs, stuffed body, blonde wig. Orinda Doll Show September, 1977. *Courtesy of Susan Hoy*

Five wax figures seen at outdoor antique and flea market show in San Juan Bautista, California, August 1977. *Courtesy of Margie Schuck Antiques — Santa Ana, Cal.*

Early 12" papier-mâché doll, stuffed with straw. Note Kathe Kruse doll behind doll on the left, in plastic for $145. *Courtesy Susan Hoy*

forty years longer. The rather lethargic wax doll heads to that date were not internationally admired, but the Montanari dolls with their pink complexions (sometimes painted and sometimes colored in the wax), the portraiture modeling, and dark ringlets changed all this, and the dolls seemed to come alive.

Also famed for beautiful wax dolls was the Pierotti family who migrated to England from Italy in 1780. Dominico Pierotti was the first Pierotti to be recognized as a wax doll modeler and this craft was carried through the family for 155 years, ending in 1935. The Pierotti dolls have been described as looking happier than the Montanari dolls, and have a darker pink complexion. These dolls, also, were never mass produced. Very often the Montanari and Pierotti dolls were not marked, and one might need an expert to confirm authenticity.

The most unique characteristic of the Montanari and Pierotti dolls is that they are not reinforced with a harder material, such as papier-mâché or composition. Although the Montanari dolls were of thicker wax, both can be held up to the light and the rays will shine through. The heads and limbs of the dolls were made by pouring liquid wax into molds, letting it form a skin, and then draining off the residue. Often this was done several times, with color going into the wax to produce a beautiful life-like tone.

In the 1860s some wax dolls had painted bonnets and coiffures molded onto their heads. Leather hands and movable arms of wax also came into use.

n the 1870s the hair of the wax dolls was modeled in pompadour fashion, over which wigs were sometimes placed, which were made of human hair or mohair. Wax dolls with molded pompadours (often with a black band around the hair) were called Squash Heads. By this time, wax dolls were as popular as china dolls, although they were destined to be replaced by the bisques.

England, France and Germany were well into the wax-doll business by the 1880s, although the wax-over-papier-mâché was more extensively used. The stuffed straw bodies had voice boxes and the dolls were provided with pierced ears. The limbs were either composition or wood. Fortunately, these dolls could be restored by rewaxing. Until 1880, the majority of dolls had closed lips, but soon they began to appear with inserted teeth, sometimes made of wood peg.

The Germans were able to mass produce these dolls, which caused a flood of cheaper versions and from the northern border of Bavaria, wax dolls streamed profusely to other ports. Papier-mâché reinforced dolls of wax were much more durable. The papier-mâché was cooked and molded with powdered clay and glue until it reached the consistency of dough. This doughlike substance was then rolled and cut into square pieces, which were pressed into molds. The eyes were set in and attached to a wire and chips were sometimes used to fill the cavity. The dried head was then painted reddish orange and dunked several times in boiling wax. The reddish orange color beneath the wax gave the doll a slightly pink complexion. Cheeks, lips, eyebrows, and pink-lined nostrils were then added. Glossy blonde mohair curls or individually rooted hair completed the doll head. White calico, pastel kid or pliable sheepskin bodies stuffed with sawdust were added.

In 1881 Fritz Bartenstein of Germany patented a movable double-faced doll head which was made of poured beeswax. One face was smiling, the other crying. One side of the head was always hidden in an attached hood or cap, and the faces were changed with the pulling of a string from the side of the body. The string was also attached to a bellow-type crier.

No old wax dolls are found in bargain places to-

All-original 9½" papier-mâché milliner "Bertha." Original enamel paint, wood arms and legs, 1820-1850.
Courtesy of Joseph Cleary

10" Chinese papier-mâchés. Marked: Michael Lee/Chinese Character Doll No. 10/ 571 Micole. (Right) Groom with hat made in Hong Kong. No. 6, Micole Siao san tac. (Left) Doll with pony tail, wearing plaid jacket and black trousers. Stuffed torso, papier-mâché head, feet, arms ¾ papier-mâché, painted features. $20 at doll show. *Courtesy Norma Quinn*

day. We are fortunate to find them in doll shops or doll shows. Sometimes being at the right place at the right time when a privately owned collection is being sold can yield a rather rare doll to add to our own collections. Some members of the National Institute of American Doll Artists (NIADA) presently working in wax are Guy & Virginia Elliot, Florence Colorado; Gladys MacDowell, Fairfax, Virginia; Irma Park, Buena Park, California; and Lewis Sorensen, Fullerton, California.

Fortunately, the author was able to find some wax figures for sale at a recent outdoor antique/flea market in San Juan Bautista, California and the owner graciously allowed the dolls to be photographed.

P A P I E R - M Â C H É

Papier-mâché is a substance made of pulped paper mixed with glue and other materials; or layers of paper glued or pressed together when moist to form various articles that become strong and hard when dry.

Papier-mâché and wax mediums came into being almost simultaneously and the overlapping of these

Close-up of three small wax figures. Smaller figures priced at $25, larger $40. *Courtesy of Margie Schuck Antiques, Santa Ana, California.*

two products brings them together in this chapter as almost inseparable products.

It is believed that the use of papier-mâché was first practiced in China, and soon spread to France and Germany. In the fifteenth century papier-mâché was used by sculptors and well into the eighteenth century busts and statues were still being made of it. Many Italian artifacts have been found made of papier-mâché and all of us are familiar with highly colored and glazed trinket boxes and trays of this material.

By the 1870s papier-mâché articles were being made by the simplest of methods—sheets of paper were laid over one another and pasted firmly on a model; or a clay and fiber compound was kneaded and rolled into sheets by steam pressure. However, 1820 is the year first noted for dolls made of papier-mâché. Between 1820 and 1830 Germany massed produced these doll heads, which were attached to kid or cotton bodies. Many of the old papier-mâché dolls are seen with a molded Queen Victoria-type hairdo, with braids on each side of the face coming down from the side and under the ears, to be joined to a braided coil in back.

At the same Great Exhibition in London for which Augusta Montanari was recognized for her wax dolls, Japanese and Chinese papier-mâché baby dolls with movable joints were on show. The heads were painted and dipped in wax. Some of the papier-mâché heads were covered with a glaze to preserve the exterior finish. Japanese and Chinese figures are still being made today with a papier-mâché base, covered with a creamy white stucco, which has been used since the turn of the century.

Ludwig Greiner of Philadelphia was a German immigrant who made the papier-mâché doll an unforgettable part of the parade of dolls. His dolls became so famous that old papier-mâché dolls are often referred to as pre-Greiner or post-Greiner. His dolls had ornate hair styles and in spite of their excellent modeling did not have glass eyes, as previously believed, but painted eyes. Greiner made the heads only and homemade bodies were attached to them. Greiner applied for a patent first in 1858 and again in 1872. The Greiner dolls had the projecting areas of the doll's face (such as the nose and chin) reinforced with linen or muslin saturated with

The two dolls in the foreground are papier-mâché milliners' models. The doll on the right is 9". (Left, rear) A French Rohner bisque. (Right, rear) 19½" milliner, $875. Doll show in Orinda, California, September 1977. *Courtesy of D. Christenson of Ross, California*

Three dolls recently found at inside flea market. Papier-mâché couple, stuffed bodies, $52. Wax doll on right approximately 10", from Switzerland. *Courtesy of Jetta Dunn, Red Barn, Aromas, California*

paste. He also strengthened the seams in this manner, cementing or pasting muslin, linen or silk to those areas. The Greiner labels were black and gold, but students of Greiner dolls can tell them at almost an instant glance. Greiner advertised the dolls as being finished with oiled paint and his were the first noted American-made papier-mâché dolls.

Two other papier-mâché dolls of note are the milliner dolls, both in dressmaker and hairdresser models, which carried the latest styles to England and the United States. Nearly all of the early papier-mâché dolls had molded hair, and were five to thirty-six inches in height. Since china dolls were popular at the same time, the hair and styling of the dolls were often similar. They had stiff, jointless kid bodies and crude wooden arms and legs. The M & S Superior doll was also an important part of the papier-mâché doll story. The M & S Superior doll bodies were stuffed and the gowning of these dolls made them recognizable in their striped stockings and buttoned leather shoes. Milliner and M & S Superior dolls date from between 1820 and 1860.

The tumbling Daruma doll is a symbolic doll on a circular base with weighted end. It is saying "Stand up little priest, for Buddha cannot fall." The story behind the doll is that an Indian priest brought

Buddhism to Japan and in A.D. 400 he moved to China, where he spent nine years in meditation with his entire body wrapped against the cold. In Tokyo the doll may be sold without eyes. If a wish made by the owner should come true, one eye is painted, and the second eye is painted only when another wish comes true. Most of the bases of the Daruma dolls are of papier-mâché, although the heads might be either gesso, mask, or papier-mâché.

The use of papier-mâché has overlapped into the composition manufacture of dolls, which will be discussed in the next chapter. Today novice doll artists still fashion dolls from papier-mâché, but the process is much simpler than the old method of cooking the paper, beating it, and pressing it into sheets. One need only go to an art supply store to find instant papier-mâché. With the addition of water, the substance immediately becomes malleable; drying can be accelerated by heating the finished model in a home oven at 150°-350°. These doll heads, made in any fashion desired by the modeler, are then coated with primer, painted with poster or tempera colors, and then finished with a varnish of clear plastic glaze.

6" Dancing Scotsman with wind-up key in back, one-piece body and legs, head and shoulders glued on body, painted features. No marks. Bargained down at flea market from $4 to $2.

7" Darumas, painted press masked faces; body, weighted papier-mâché. Bargained down from $20 to $10 pair.
Courtesy Norma Quinn

chapter 5

Dolls Of Wood

Wooden dolls have been bounced and toted about for centuries, bundled up and sold by wandering salesmen as early as the fifteenth century. The prowess of the German and Austrian wood carvers was already known and soon they were joined by the English and Dutch craftsmen who were also engrossed in the making of doll houses and miniature furniture. Although wood likenesses have been exhumed from ancient graves, they no doubt had a religious connotation rather than being playthings. By 1800, wood toys out sold those of brass and tin and Austrian, French, and German wood carvers had brought their talents to worldwide attention.

It is interesting to note that many of the early wooden dolls were embossed with a doughlike substance, later referred to as plaster of Paris or gesso. Perhaps it was simpler to embellish the dolls with curls and bosoms made of an easy-to-mold substance, rather than enduring the painstaking process of carving curls and curves. Queen Anne dolls (named after Queen Anne of England 1665—1714) often had thin plaster coatings and dolls of this period had, besides the usual painted black hair, wigs of human hair or flax. The Queen Anne dolls had inset glass eyes and were fashionably gowned in elaborate ensembles more intricate in detail than the doll itself. The gesso or plaster coverings over the wooden dolls of this period were covered with coats of colorful paint, sometimes highly varnished, and the design of the doll body had progressed to wooden ball joints. Tracks of small dots were painted to represent the eyebrows and lashes.

Dolls of wood became famous as the English pedlar dolls of the mid-eighteenth century. Much has been written about the pedlar dolls of England, named after their human counterparts, the "notion nannies" of England who travelled about the countryside selling their wares. These pedlar dolls were the delight of the socially elite, as well as the peasants who made them, and were often housed in dust-proof glass cases in the wealthy English homes. Most of the pedlar dolls were eight to ten inches in height, wore a white mob hat which fitted down over the ears (often worn indoors by Englishwomen) and cloaked in a bright-red hooded cape. The printed peasant gowns were accented with crisp white aprons. These dolls carried a tray containing "notions" including tin toys, sewing and household knickknacks and even fortune notes. Although it is rare indeed to find an authentic old pedlar doll today, our modern artists have begun devoting their talents to re-establishing this category of doll and embellishing their trays with both old and modern notions. . . a good challenge for collectors of old thimbles, buttons and miniatures.

While leafing through an issue of *Doll Castle News*, I was delighted to find an article by Jean Bach of Raggedy Ann Antique & Toy Museum about a comtemporary artist, Marie Costello, who, quite by accident and through a series of fascinating events, came to fashion a wooden pedlar doll. Always creative, Marie was charmed by a picture of an antique doll in a book and began to create a doll from wooden parts that her son had purchased. As she researched the pedlar doll, Marie began to design a doll clothed in authentic fashion. Every doll has a handmade human hair wig and the clothing is designed and handmade by Marie. Marie, her husband Thomas, her daughters Jenny and Jeanne and her son Michael all participated in the making of these beautiful dolls.

Many of the pedlar dolls were made of wood, although there were also some pedlars of papier-mâché, wax, china, and composition. Recently a delightful pedlar doll made from bread dough was seen and, of course, apple dolls and stuffed dolls can also be fashioned into pedlars.

The most famous English wooden dolls (imported from the Netherlands) are those brightly-colored wood creations with simple features that were so loved by Princess Victoria, who became queen of England in 1837. The princess had a priceless collection—132 dolls. These simple dolls three to nine inches tall were chosen by the princess over others that might have been more elaborately modeled. The tiny dolls with sharp little noses, molded black hair that was accented in the back with a small comb and greyish curls subduing the sharp middle part in front, must have appealed especially to the young girl. The princess was allowed to attend plays and operas of the Kensington choice, and from these touches of human contact, the princess and her governess gowned the dolls to represent theatrical stars. Until she was fourteen, the princess held

Handmade pedlar doll by Marie Costello. Wood head, stuffed cotton body and arms, painted features. Mounted on wood stand which is stamped "handcrafted by Marie A. Costello, Easton, Pa." Tray contains miniature bell, rolling pin, spools of thread, beads, small basket with miniature tools, plus miniatures hanging in front of wooden tray. Basket on left arm contains flour and grain. Left arm also holds broom and skeins of yarn. On right arm is crocheted holder for bread loaves. Doll itself is approximately 14", plus stand. $40 purchased through Raggedy Ann Doll Museum, Flemington, New Jersey.

securely to her wooden dolls as her warmest friends and companions.

Wooden dolls were not always entirely composed of wood. Some had cloth arms and legs, sometimes leather-jointed, with heads of china, wax, or papier-mâché. Carved bamboo or simple straw hands were often attached to a doll head of wood. Even rag bodies sometimes carried a wooden head, although the weight must have created some problems. Early in the 1800s the bust and hair were often carved into elaborate fashions. The peg wooden dolls, which simply had pegs inserted at the shoulder and hip joints to allow easy movement, were most prevalent in the smallest of the dolls. The New England "penny" dolls of the mid 1800s ran from less than one to twelve inches in height with tiny waists, swan necks, and lovely sloping shoulders and sold for the grand price of one cent.

By the early twentieth century, hand-carved wooden dolls were being imported into America from Germany and Holland. Possibly the first commercially manufactured wooden dolls in America were the Joel Ellis dolls, made of kiln-dried rock maple with hands and feet of iron. In 1873 Joel Ellis received a patent for these mortise and tenon jointed dolls which were held with steel pins and could be moved into several acrobatic poses. Steamed and softened maple wood was hydraulically pressed into the proper steel molds for the dolls' head, while bodies and limbs were turned on a lath. Joel Ellis dolls have painted black iron shoes, with the hands painted either black or white. The head, including the shoulder, and the limbs were dipped in flesh-tone paint. The timberland near Springfield, Vermont was nurtured by the Black River and the abundance of fine wood helped both Joel Ellis and Luke Taylor, another dollmaker/mechanic of Springfield, Vermont, to have ample supplies of the rock maple from which their dolls emerged. Both floods and the economic depression of 1873 forced Joel Ellis to disband his doll-making venture, but his creative capabilities were not completely stunted, for the Joel Ellis baby carriages earned him the nickname "Cab" Ellis. (These grand creations are further discussed in chapter X.)

Luke Taylor lived in Springfield at the same time as Joel Ellis, and their acquaintance no doubt in-

8" wood doll with tag stating "an exact replica of the famous antique New England Museum model." By Shackman, N.Y. Made in Japan. Flea market price, 50 cents.

spired some of the fine craftsmanship for which
Springfield will be forever known. The Mason and
Taylor dolls (1879-1882) derived their name from
Henry Mason, a travelling salesman of acute awareness who supplied Luke Taylor with ideas upon his
return from trips through the countryside. It was he
who asked Luke Taylor to design the doll which had
a body of soft wood, with limbs of rock maple or
hardwood beech. In 1871, these partners invented a
jointed neck, held together by an iron pin which fitted tightly into a wooden groove. Wooden spoon
hands (later replaced with pewter) and painted blue
feet further distinguish these dolls that were covered
with gesso.

Albert Schoenhut, son of Frederick Schoenhut
and grandson of Anton Wilhelm Schoenhut, was the
third generation of a talented family of wood
toymakers. But Albert, determined not to become
just another toymaker, came to the United States at
the age of seventeen. Other members of his family
(brothers) followed, and became involved in the
Schoenhut Toy Company, specializing in musical
toys. Perhaps Albert did not consciously realize he
was returning to his natural talents when he made a
small wooden piano for a friend, but the news soon
spread and requests poured in for more pianos. In
1909 Albert Schoenhut applied for a patent for a
wooden doll and by 1911 he was commercially in the
business. The Schoenhut dolls were all wood and
their spring tension joints and steel spring hinges
made them fully articulated. The wrist and ankle
joints, and feet were often of hardwood. The head
was made of basswood on the end of the grain, and
the character-faced Schoenhuts soon were replaced
by regular doll faces with movable wooden eyes.
Several coats of oil enamel were applied over the
wood. Because the dolls were advertised as
washable, the children did just that, and so, today,
Schoenhuts are often lacking the original painted
surfaces. Even unwashed, some Schoenhuts suf-
fered surface cracking and chipping. Often the doll
had molded hair, but mohair wigs were also used extensively. The feet, shoes and stockings all were
made with holes in the bottom to accommodate the
metal stands of the spring-jointed Schoenhuts.

Schoenhut dolls can be found today, but the
prices are in the $200—$500 range, and are sure to

Shoenhut wood girl in beautiful condition.
Found at Orinda doll show in 1977.
Courtesy of Marion Cleary

6" all wood Dutch doll. Gray mohair wig, painted features, Dutch wooden shoes, stick legs painted black, attached to body with nail. $2 in flea market.

rise. This is quite a jump from the original $2—$5 price. Even small Schoenhut dolls, such as a nine-inch black boy is valued at $90 today, and a 4-inch Roly-Poly sells for a similar price. If a collector should show you a Schoenhut and your eyes do not widen with surprise and shock, it is whispered as though a secret: "It's a Schoenhut".

The famous Schoenhut circus characters are coveted by all, especially the small-doll collectors. There are animals, ring masters, and clowns, for instance, jointed by rubber cord to allow realistic positioning of the bodies. An unnamed stranger sold the rights to Schoenhut for the circus figures for a mere hundred dollars, disregarding Albert's urgings to produce them on his own.

As the pressure to produce less expensive dolls began to effect the manufacture of Schoenhut dolls in the early 1920s, the quality had to be sacrificed and the dolls were changed for the worse by having joints strung with elastic cord. Stuffed dolls with mama voices were advertised as zealously as the original Schoenhuts, but sales dropped off. In 1935 the Philadelphia factory was liquidated. Some rare Schoenhuts that were not hailed as anything unusual at the time are now vigorously sought by collectors. They are the mannequin dolls manufactured for commercial display, and the copies of the head of Grace Putnam's Bye-Low baby.

As descendents of the brave pioneers that headed West in covered wagons loaded with dreams, there is one American wooden doll that we can most closely relate to. The doll referred to is Patty Reed's Doll—the wooden doll that was the lone survivor of the fateful Donner Party who travelled the brutal trail from Springfield, Illinois, to Sutter's Fort, California, suffering the ravages of the cold winter of 1846—47. In the book *Patty Reed's Doll* by Rachel Kelley Laurgaard, the 4-inch wooden dolly with a "knob of painted (black) hair", rosy cheeks and wooden joints tells the story of the American families who encountered frustration, sorrow, hunger and fear before they reached the promised land of sunshine and flowers—California. Author Laurgaard extensively researched the story of Patty's doll, and the material which she elicited from the history of the Donner Party provides the background for the story of one little girl's love for her doll, and her determination to hold on to the one precious part of her childhood belongings.

The dolly, first carried about in Patty's apron pocket, soon became a stow-away hidden under Patty's blouse when precious belongings had to be abandoned on the trail, including Patty's beautiful doll family with their "fragile faces" and beautiful velvet clothes. At one point, the dolly nearly fell victim to the trash heap too, as Patty bent down to pick up a little glass doll dish and play silverware and the dolly fell out of her pocket. However, Patty "snatched me up quickly and hid me in the lining of her waist, fearing, I suppose, that should her mother know she had me, I too would be taken away from her." As the pioneer families fought their way over the Sierra mountains, Patty reassures her dolly (whose wooden body protected her from "skeeter bites") that Papa Reed would come right over the mountains to rescue them and bring them "Johnny-cakes and cookies" so that they would never be hungry again.

After the long ordeal ended, the dolly relates "And so I stayed with Patty always. She could not bear to part with me after all we shared together. We had been pioneers across the plains and mountains and deserts to California, and in that long year since we had left Springfield, we had known the worst suffering that pioneers can know."

"Patty grew up and had a family of her own. She kept me carefully in a box of relics in her bureau drawer. A lock of grandma's hair wrapped up in lace, a little knife and fork and spoon, and a tiny

4½" wood bride and groom, 1940s. Legs are clothespin tops and wire. Painted features, mohair wigs. Bride is in white satin with pink and blue flowers in bouquet as well as trim on net veil. Groom is in black top and white trousers, black felt bow tie. Marks on box: DOLL HOUSE, Clothes Pin Dolls are Original, Handmade and Movable. Manufactured by Woodcraft Studios, 493 Wabasha St., St. Paul 2, Minn. Inside flea market price, $10; bargained down to $5. *Photo by Roger Fremier*

glass dish she had picked up that day when I fell out of her pocket on the desert . . . all lay beside me on her father's big mitten which had concealed the crumbs that saved her life. Now and then she opened the box and allowed her children, and then her grandchildren, to caress me with their soft fingers. . ."

Of her doll, Patty said "she is very precious to me—my oldest friend."

In 1947 Patty Reed's doll arrived at Sutter's Fort in Sacramento, California, where she can now be seen in the museum, accompanied by a note from Patty. "Money—not even all the gold of California could replace this little piece of wood . . .". There is also a very accurate copy of the Patty Reed doll at Donner Memorial State Park.

And so the simple wooden dollies have become a faithful and precious part of our history. Although today many can be seen in museums, there are still simple dolls of wood that we can find and hold as our very own until they too pass on to future generations.

Another group of colorful, awesome dolls of wood are the American Indian Kachina dolls. Although it seems somehow that the Kachina dolls, with their religious connotations, belong only to the American Indians and their spiritual gods, many collectors find their beauty and symbolism too endear-

Modern wood nest dolls and bouncy-head Kokeshi, Japan. Nest dolls in both Japanese and Russian dress can still be found in stores today for $5 and for only $3 at flea markets, 50 cents for Kokeshi dolls.

ing to pass by. Although it is questionable whether a "non-Indian" ever really purchases a truly authentic Kachina doll, they are very appealing, and certainly should be mentioned as dolls which are an important part of the American heritage.

The Kachinas belong to the Hopi Indians, who live on the high mesas of north central Arizona. The Kachina doll symbolizes the spiritual world which is contacted by the Hopi Kachina dancers during their ceremonial dances. The dolls are three to thirty-six inches in height and were originally colored with earth paints, but now the masks and bodies are brightly adorned with poster paint of many colors.

The lifestyle of the Hopi Indians is reflected in the adornments of the Kachina dancers. The dancers may be adorned with bags of cornmeal, green corn stalks, and feathers from not only the eagle, but the macaw and turkey. They may be garbed in furs and the masks may be modeled with horns, yucca leaves, and intricate geometric designs carried over from their pottery and jewelry. Bells may jangle from the breasts of the dancers and keep the rhythm on the ankles of their dancing feet.

Many travelers have witnessed the Hopi dances (December through August) on the six thousand foot plateaus where the Hopi make their home. The observers sitting in designated places soon understand the Indian belief that the dancers lose their human identity during the dance and become the Kachina spirit which carries messages from their people to the gods of rain and harvest and happiness. During the ceremonies, the Kachina dolls are passed to the Hopi children as a ritual of remembrance and appreciation of their spiritual beliefs.

Many persons visiting the Soviet Union have brought back with them the matreshka or nest dolls. It is great fun to play with these dolls, popping off each outer cover to find another small doll inside, until at last there is a teeny doll—the last treasure to be found. Some of the matreshkas have up to twelve dolls inside. By 1900 these dolls were exhibited in Paris and in 1958 they were part of the Brussels Fair. The matreshkas are known to have come to Russia from the Far East; as early in 1900 there were sets of these dolls in China. These dolls are still being produced both in Russia and the Far East. At a local toy shop a small set (five dolls) sells for five dollars.

Two Kachina dolls mounted in picture frames. At flea market and antique show for $50 each. *Courtesy of Betty Shapard*

The doll is painted as a typical peasant with cloak and headscarf. The contemporary Japanese sets are also obtainable today in the stores.

The bouncy headed wooden kokeshi dolls are known to have been produced as a folk art in Japan for several years. The myriad of shapes and colors can be a fascinating and inexpensive type of doll to collect.

The two wooden dolls from Turkey in illustration were purchased at an outdoor antique/flea market in the summer of 1977. The head, body, and limbs were thought to be wood, and although quite primitive, were considered charming and worthy of collection. (However, close examination is not always possible in on-the-spot transactions, since sellers frown at complete unfrocking and pulling and tugging of joints for a closer look at their dolls.) Although the flea market seller believed the dolls to be from the 1930s, the red plastic shoes and hands (which at first glance resembled composition or papier-mâché) would place the dolls more realistically into at least the 1940s. The heads were attached to the wood block torsos by only a nail. A fleck of paint chipped from the neck of one doll revealed an almost too-red color for wood and the pressure of a fingernail made a small indentation which sprung back to its original shape. The heads were made of rubber! Painted with a flesh-colored dull paint, they closely resembled wood with only bumps and small

Jumping Jack found in junk shop for 50 cents, selling in retail stores for $3.00. Small wood doll with painted cheeks from Switzerland. Purchased in group of dolls at flea market for 25 cents.

Hand-carved wood miniatures by Matt
Blomfield of Knoxville, Tennessee. Pedlar
and "Hitty" about 8" tall. *Photo by
Joe Marshall; courtesy of Helen Bullard*

hollows used to denote facial features. The bright
shine of the eyes and lips makes one suspect that
they are painted decals, but rather than completely
confirm this suspicion by removing any of the facial
decorations, it is better to be content with only the
suspicion. Bosoms were made by two brass tacks,
only slightly pressed into the wood, and the entire
torso was softened by sponge rubber padding. The
mobility of the stick arms and legs was accomplished
by using wooden pegs. There is a combination of
hand and machine sewing in the clothing, which
always makes one curious about the makers of these
crude but charming dolls. Connoisseurs of hand-
carved wooden dolls might scoff that the cheap
manner in which these dolls were assembled is quite
evident; but they have been admired by many collectors and the very distinction of being primitively
contrived by some elusive stranger in another land
makes them well worth the small price and short
span of time spent to get acquainted.

A leisurely stroll through today's toy shops
reveals very few dolls of wood. The soft plastic dolls
that burp, and creep, and cry, and talk seem to better
hold the   attention of our young offspring. Only
three charming wooden dolls were found. On their
wooden feet is a sticker simply marked *Made in
Poland*.

Fortunately, our doll artists are perpetuating the beauty and artistry of the wooden dolls. Pictured in illustration are three dolls created, carved and costumed by Helen Bullard of Ozone, Tennessee, founder of NIADA (National Institute of American Doll Artists). They are called Alice in Wonderland Fantasy, and I am grateful to her for graciously sending this picture of her dolls to share with us all. Helen is an internationally recognized artist who sculptures in a light colored hardwood, horse-chestnut. The character of each piece of chestnut is allowed to naturally control the completed doll form. Helen's dolls, in their modern simplicity, show both personality and attitude, which is further reinforced by careful costuming. In the Oakridge Children's Museum eighteen of Helen's carved figures, depicting an American family covering nine generations, can be seen. Her interest in creating hand carved dolls began in 1949. Her first doll, named after her daughter's imaginary playmate, Holly, was in the form of a little mountain girl. Since that time, this artist has had many successes, having written six books, was elected first president of NIADA in 1962 and fortunately for those who appreciate beautifully carved dolls, Helen Bullard is still sculpturing dolls from chestnut logs, slabs and posts.

Wooden dolls, through the centuries, have steadfastly refused to be anything but faithful and durable. With their knack for becoming famous, who knows to what heights the next wooden dolls will reach.

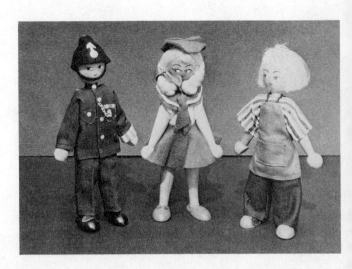

Three 7¼" wood dolls found in toy shop in 1977 for $2 each. Made in Poland decal on shoe.

Hopi Kachina Harvest Dancer, 1950s, holding ears of corn. 9½" white one-piece wood body; arms, legs painted with green and black; fur around ankles; feather atop head; mask of white, gray, gold, and black; green yarn at neck. $30 at flea market and antique show.

Doll artist, Helen Bullard, created, carved, and costumed these outstanding dolls, part of an *Alice in Wonderland* fantasy, ranging in size 2", 18", 6½". *Photo by Joe Marshall; courtesy of Helen Bullard*

Back view of same Kachina dancer.

8" dolls from Turkey, 1940s. Combination of wood, rubber, and plastic, with foam padding. $7.50 a pair at flea market.

chapter 6

Composition, Celluloid, and Rubber Dolls

The smallest of the composition Ideal Shirley Temple dolls, 11" size, all original. Light blue (now nearly white) dress with pink ribbon at waist, neckline, and hair; panties attached to white slip; pink socks, white shoes; blonde mohair wig. Tag on dress reads: Genuine Shirley Temple Doll, Registered U.S. Pat. Off., Ideal Novelty & Toy Co., Made in USA. Head and body both marked 11/Shirley Temple. Price is $125 at outside antique show.

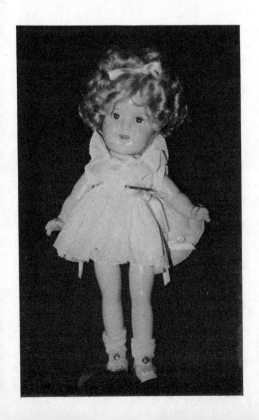

Those of us who are constantly scanning the bargain centers for dolls are delighted to chance upon the old and familiar composition dolls from the 1920s and 30s. These composition dolls bring back happy memories for someone in nearly every family today, whether it be grandmother, mother, or daughter. From the beginning of this century through the 1940s, composition remained a stable part of the doll industry. In the heyday of the 1930s-40s they brought us famous dolls such as Shirley Temple, Sonja Henie, Judy Garland, Jane Withers, Princess Elizabeth, Scarlett O'Hara, the Dionne quintuplets, and a myriad of others. However, they didn't need to be representations of popular stars, but the lovable compos suited us just fine as loyal and durable companions. (I am forever watching for my old doll with orange molded hair and a loop in the head for a ribbon.)

Some fortunate collectors have in their possession today, composition dolls produced in the last decades of the 1800s, but a doll made entirely of composition in this period is quite rare and not easily available to us all.

The concept of composition was developed nearly fifty years before the turn of the century, quite possibly first in England, and then in Germany. By 1877, an American named Lazarus Reichman is on record as having developed a composition material and soon this inexpensive doll material was available to the masses.

It is sometimes hard to tell a papier-mâché doll from a composition doll, especially if the doll has been covered with several coats of paint. What then, went into the making of composition? Most commonly, a wood by-product was the basic ingredient and such terms as *wood flour mixture* (meaning finely powdered sawdust), *pulp mixture, sawdust* or a *rag and paper combination* have been used to describe the making of a composition product. Some companies kept their mixtures a guarded secret, but we know that glue or resin was used to hold the mixture together. Once the composition material was processed, it was placed in molds to harden, and the doll parts were then sanded and painted with enamel. Composition is usually heavier than papier-mâché and tends to have a smoother exterior.

Alexander Dionne Quints, 1936, 7" all composition with molded brown hair and painted side-glancing brown eyes. *Courtesy of Patricia Smith from Allin's collection*

A doll collector can usually recognize a composition doll without even touching it. However, plastic made at about the same time as the composition doll was tinted and molded in much the same fashion and the outward appearance (including wigs) of these plastic dolls can often fool even the experienced collector at first glance. By simply holding the doll, the heavier weight of the composition becomes evident, and if all else fails, an examination of the sockets of the dolls' arms and legs reveals the compressed mixture, often unpainted at the edges.

Some of the first composition-doll heads had a heavy wax overcoating applied to the surface. The ball-jointed composition-doll body was replaced in 1880 by the Jumeau family with a composition body strung together with elastic.

In the early 1900s, German and French firms were producing baby figures with chubby arms and legs bent into babylike positions. By the 1920s doll companies were producing character dolls that could be cuddly and ugly and fat and comical.

The most famous of the baby dolls in the 1930s were the Dionne quintuplets manufactured by the Madame Alexander Doll Company. To own all five Dionne quintuplets—Marie, Cecile, Annette, Emilie, and Yvonne—is a doll collector's dream. (If only we had saved those paper dolls bought for 10¢ at the five-and-dime!) Of special interest to the small collector are the seven-inch composition quint babies. Recently at a doll show four of the quints were seen, along with some other printed material relating to their popularity, priced at $150. The quint babies were later produced as toddlers and older children. The Ideal Toy Company produced baby Shirley Temple dolls in composition, which are very seldom seen and much sought by collectors. The dolls were

4½" Scottish bagpiper, 1930-1948. Composition, hand-painted. Germany-Riedeler firm. Figures from Nazi era included Hitler, Mussolini. $20 value each, found at garage sale for $1. *Photo by Roger Fremier*

9" composition Patsyette by Effanbee. Photographed at outdoor antique and flea market. $35.00.
*Courtesy of Maison de Poupées,
Fresno, California*

quite large, measuring sixteen to twenty-five inches.
The smallest of the Shirley Temple dolls is the
eleven-inch composition doll. She also is very rare.

Madame Alexander Doll Company produced
composition storybook dolls in the mid-30s. Ten
years later another storybook series in composition
was made up of nine-inch Hollywood dolls. A small-
doll collector may have to search awhile to find
small dolls of composition, but they do exist; which
is part of the joy of doll collecting—to find the unusual and rare dolls. There are a number of adorable
small babies in composition, often unmarked,
colored black, brown, and white, that certainly add
much to a doll collection. There are still parts available from collectors and doll hospitals for the composition dolls, so buying one that is missing a limb is
a rather safe gamble.

As fond as we are of our composition dolls, they
are not without fault. The surface of the composition, unless it has been kept carefully wrapped and
stored in a temperate place, nearly always shows
crackle or crazing of the enameled surface. In extreme cases, the enamel will crack open and chip off.
When a lovely composition doll is seen baking in the
sun on a flea market table, my first instinct is to
rescue the doll, regardless of price, before the heat of
the day crumbles its fragile exterior. However, it is
not possible to save all the dolls, no matter how good
the intentions, and all that can be hoped for is a continuing awareness of how old dolls should be preserved.

1934 calendar showing the five
Dionne Quints, $5 at collector shop.
London Baking Company Ad

Doll collectors disagree about the crazing or crackle lines on composition dolls. Many of the collectors feel that if the doll is in otherwise good condition, a few crackle lines helps to confirm the age of the doll and gives it character that a doll of that era should have; others prefer to have the lines removed. However, be cautious about purchasing a composition doll with the thought in mind of restoring it to like new condition, for restoring composition dolls is very expensive. The repair of a composition doll head may cost as much as the doll is worth. It is a major repair because the doll must be stripped, sanded, and repainted with several coats of enamel. The facial features must then be redone and if the doll has molded hair, it must be repainted also. Repair to a composition doll should be done by experts. Many well-meaning doll owners have either washed away the doll's facial features or ruined the enamel coating by attempting home repairs. The doll's surface may be preserved longer by gently rubbing the surface with baby oil. It does not seem to harm the doll to apply a creamy face makeup on areas that have faded. Do not attempt to paint the doll. Nothing is more horrifying than to see a prized composition doll painted with ordinary paint.

In order to preserve your expensive old dolls, the first priority of any doll collector should be a glass enclosed china cabinet—both for display and to keep the dust and dirt from penetrating the doll and doll clothing. However, the price of lovely large china cabinets is quite prohibitive and I fear many of us procrastinate and stuff our dolls in boxes, trunks, dresser drawers, closets, and other hidden spots in the house, or we display them in the open and console ourselves with the thought that we will soon obtain an enclosed cabinet. One of my standby answers to the familiar question, "Where will you put any more dolls in the house?" is "I still have a whole attic to go."

The value of composition dolls is rising sharply and those "stars" of the composition years are superseded in price only by the old bisque, china, and wax dolls. Prices may start at $2-$5 for a rather broken, shabby composition doll (but with character!) to $275 for a Shirley Temple. Princess Elizabeths by Madame Alexander Toy Company were seen recently in a California doll show with prices of $75-$160.

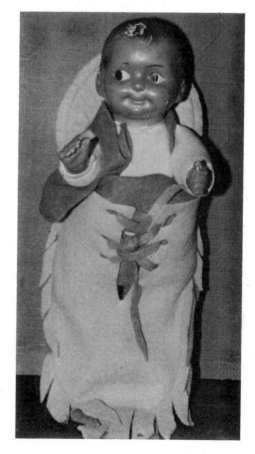

9" composition Indian papoose, about 1917. Torso stuffed with straw, arms attached to body with metal disc, swaddled in felt blanket.
Courtesy of Norma Quinn

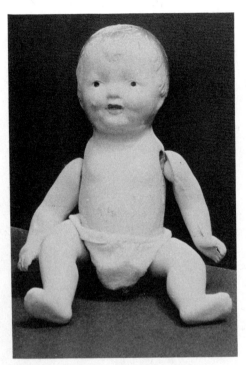

8¾" composition baby. Molded hair, painted features, strung arms and legs. No marks.
Courtesy of Lois Meade Harbert

9" composition baby. Painted features, molded hair. No marks. Purchased at flea market for $2.00 in 1977.

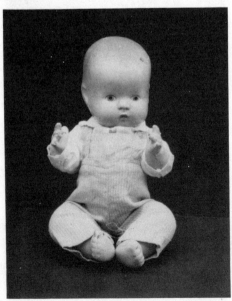

One factor in favor of the collector searching for composition dolls is that they can still be found at garage sales, flea markets, and some rummage sales. Collectible shops and some antique stores also have composition dolls tucked in the corners. The composition dolls are tomorrow's antiques and many can still be picked up for a few dollars today. Future doll collectors will thank us for saving these lovely dolls from the junk pile!

CELLULOID

Who doesn't remember the feathered and spangled carnival dolls, dangling enticingly from wooden sticks along the carnival midway? It was always a toss-up whether to get the fuzzy monkey or the doll, but of course the doll always won. These big-eyed celluloid cuties were composed of thin celluloid, and small owners soon discovered that the tiny hollow bodies would crackle and crunch at the slightest pressure. How hopeless it was to try and fix the dent by pinching somewhere else to make it "pop" out.

Parkesine was the first name given to this material, created by Englishman Alexander Parkes, who was looking for a suitable substitute for ivory. Some of the fine celluloid dolls do indeed look like ivory, with their delicate painted heads. By 1880 an American named John W. Hyatt had experimented and developed celluloid to the point that dolls could be fashioned from celluloid sheets that had been placed under hydraulic pressure. He used pyroxylin (cellulose nitrate) plasticized with camphor and solvent. It was named celluloid, which began merely as a trademark, but the name stuck and was used ever after for any doll made of a cellulose material.

The shape of the celluloid dolls was created by blowing hot air into the molds with tanks of compressed air. Some of the early Hyatt celluloid dolls were one piece, and were produced by John Hyatt and his brother Isaiah in their Celluloid Novelty Company factory in Newark, New Jersey. If only the doll head was made of celluloid, more than likely the body was stuffed cotton. As the manufacture of celluloid dolls progressed, they were soon fashioned into jointed dolls having glass eyes and open mouths with teeth. In 1903 Kammerer and Reinhardt manufactured a sleep-eyed celluloid doll.

Since celluloid dolls became popular shortly after the bisque dolls, many of the bisque molds were used. Germany was quick to take up the celluloid doll craze.

Early in 1900 Kestner was using his bisque-doll molds to produce both celluloid heads and limbs for his well-known dolls. This celluloid was a thicker, stronger material than the later celluloids and when finished in cream tones the Kestner dolls of celluloid rivaled the beauty of the best of dolls. A large seventeen-inch Kestner doll with celluloid head was purchased recently at a doll show. This doll from the early 1900s has a finely proportioned celluloid head with raised eyebrows painted dark brown. It has the original brunette human-hair wig, brown sleep eyes, and an open mouth with four teeth. Incised on the head are the markings: *J.D.K./201./4*. The lower half of the arms are of bisque (some Kestner dolls had celluloid arms also), and the body is of white kid. At another doll show in the fall of 1977, a celluloid head was found marked with the well-known turtle, meaning it was manufactured by the Rheinische Gummi Und Celluloid Fabrik Company of Bavaria. This 3½-inch head has molded hair and painted features. Above the turtle is the word *Germany* and below the turtle *Schulz-Marke* (meaning "trademark" in German). this well known company also made celluloid dolls for well known companies like Kestner. The Rheinische Gummi Und Celluloid Fabrik Company was founded in 1873 and operated until the 1920s, using the turtle mark to mark the durable, dependable products from their factory.

11" composition doll in original wedding dress. Closed mouth, painted features. Tag on arm "Dream World Dolls Make Dreams Come True." $20 at inside flea market.

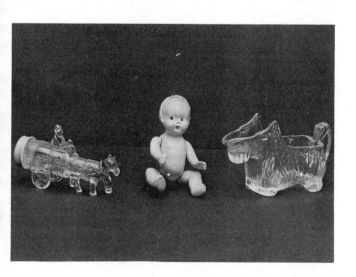

5½" unmarked 1930s composition baby. Painted features, molded red hair, pictured with candy and syrup containers shaped like "Fala," the Scotty dog of President Franklin D. Roosevelt. Cost $3 at outside flea market, value $7.50.

The Bye-Low babies often had hands made of celluloid and some of the first sleeping eyes of American dolls were made of celluloid when other materials became scarce during World War II.

As celluloid dolls began to flood the market, they were accepted gratefully by mothers who found that these dolls could be kept clean and free from germs by frequent washing. However, the main fault of the first celluloid was its flammability. By 1907 the New Jersey Company of John Hyatt patented a fireproof celluloid and thus established what was thought to be a safe and hardy material from which to make dolls.

In the 1930s the famous Kewpie doll by Rose O'Neill was also being manufactured in celluloid (some by the Rheinische Gummi Und Celluloid Fabrik Company). When World War I forced some of the European doll companies out of trade with the U.S., American and Japanese factories produced their own version of the Kewpies.

Poland, Austria, and France are also well known for their celluloid dolls. The Adelhoid Nagler Innsbruck Doll Company manufactured some fine Austrian dolls of celluloid, standing 8½ inches in height and dressed in native costumes. These were produced in the late 1930s.

Also in the late 1930s France produced some beautiful peasant-gowned celluloid dolls. On the apron of one doll, the name *SAVOIE* is written in gold ink (an alpine area in France near the Italian border). This doll was found in an indoor flea market, and since that time several dolls manufactured by this company have been found in varying sizes. If you find one of these dolls and do not want to undress it because of the pins inserted into the doll to keep the clothing intact, the markings you can use to identify the doll are: *France*, numbers, and an Eagle head. The costumes of these dolls are particularly impressive. This particular doll with blonde wig, has a black, gold-trimmed velvet headdress with gold braided chin strap. A gold cross hangs from the neck over a gold-bodice trimmed white blouse. The black apron is accented with hand painted flowers. She is wearing a shoulder shawl of paisley print trimmed with varigated fringe and yellow rayon-type skirt trimmed in gold. The doll is strung and the black shoes and white stockings are

10½" Hummel rubber doll dressed as Bavarian boy, complete with wood ladder. Black felt hat and shoes, black cotton suit, red kerchief at neck. Wood tag marked: "Felix," original M.I. Hummel. Other side of tag, "V" with bee marked W. Goebel/ OESLAU. Found at garage sale for $2.00; Value: $60-$80.
Courtesy of Gregory Chisman

painted on. These dolls have lovely beige-rose complexions and painted eyes.

Celluloid fell out of favor again when, in the 1940s, it was declared hazardous because of its explosive base. In 1967 the manufacture of celluloid toys was stopped. Becoming quite alarmed at this information, I raised the question with a science instructor at our local college. He informed me that celluloid will indeed burn when exposed to extreme heat, but while it is not recommended for a child's toy, collectors, with reasonable care, need not worry about their celluloid dolls. Our cloth and kid-bodied dolls would also burn, and therefore the usual care we take with our dolls should be sufficient.

RUBBER

As many of us who have rubber dolls in our collection know, they deteriorate quite easily, no matter what we do. Rubber dolls will crackle, paint will peel off, they will slump, and finally break open. However, because of the lovely character of the rubber dolls, we preserve them as best we can (in a cool place, dusted with powder, under glass domes or behind glass doors).

As early as the 1840s rubber doll heads were being experimented with, but would not hold their shape. By 1844 Thomas Forster had improved the use of India rubber by casting it in molds. Edward Payne, in 1849, molded and joined hollow figures into doll shapes. However, not until Charles Goodyear discovered vulcanizing (heat applied to the mixtures) did the dolls retain their shapes. In 1851 a patent was taken out by Goodyear for hard rubber.

Why were the doll manufacturers of this time concerned with rubber dolls? They were attempting to make an unbreakable doll, since the bisque and china dolls, although very lovely, brought many a tear to the eye when broken into tiny pieces. Rubber was a substance obtained from milky juices or sap from plants such as rubber trees, tropical plants, or milkweed. To increase its usefulness, crude rubber was often worked on rolls to make it more moldable and then compounded with other materials before it was molded and vulcanized.

In the late 1870s such famous doll companies as Bru and Steiner were manufacturing rubber dolls.

Composition Betty Boop 11"-12" as seen at Vallejo doll show recently. *Courtesy of Coral Cooper of Coral Cooper's Dolls, Yuba City, Calif.*

6" feathered, celluloid 1930s carnival doll with lace headband and red plastic cane. Found at flea market for $1.00, value, $7.00.

5" celluloid 1920s couple. Wigs,
painted features.
Courtesy of Mary Williams

By the 1900s, Montgomery Wards was advertising small rubber dolls. From pictures, it is evident that most of these babies had molded hair, shoes and stockings.

The author recalls Christmas of 1936 when under the tree was found the latest rubber doll—what is recalled to have been called Betsy Wetsy. It was great fun to feed the baby its bottle of water and soon find the diaper dripping wet. The doll, recently fed an entire bottle of water, was handed to Grandpa and promptly wet all over his hands. My shrieks of delight were met with Grandpa's patient smile, and although he probably soon forgot the incident, it will remain one of my most vivid memories.

Some of the most delightful dolls of rubber that can still be found today are those designed by Ruth E. Newton. They are so marked on the back of the doll's head. One of these dolls is Amosandra, the baby from the Amos and Andy radio series during the 1940s. This doll was manufactured by the Sun Rubber Company and belonged to Columbia Broadcasting System, Incorporated. At a recent doll show Amosandra was seen, in only fair condition, for eighteen dollars.

At the beginning of World War II, rubber was needed for the war effort, and so synthetic rubber evolved. Soon dolls were found with a combination of materials. Effanbee's Dy Dee Baby can still be found, and is easily recognized by the rubber ears

Two additional versions of 8" French celluloid dolls, 1939. Doll on left is dressed in gold flannel dress, cotton bonnet and shawl of pink-flowered cotton; red, black and white apron, light brown wig. Doll on right has reddish-brown wig, red felt dress, pink satin apron trimmed in same lace as bodice, gold-trimmed skirt and apron. Fancy headdress of stiffened pleated cotton, trimmed in lace. Silver star earrings pinned into head. *Roger Fremier photo*

that were applied after the hard plastic head was completed. The rubber body of this doll was manufactured by Miller Rubber Company and was produced from the 1930s until 1950. (Recent doll show price in excellent condition twenty dollars; flea market price ten dollars).

If any of you have seen dolls on the flea market tables, with lovely hard plastic heads, but arms, bodies, and legs that have turned very dark, you are looking at a doll made of the soft rubber material labeled *latex* that was quite popular in the 1940s and 50s. This latex material was called magic skin and although the other dolls of latex are not prone to this discoloring, the magic skin babies are. Any long exposure to harsh light will discolor these thin-skinned dolls. If you have a magic skin baby in good condition, it is worth saving, since they are now hard to find. Most of these dolls were stuffed with cotton or other soft filling and the bodies were usually one piece. The hands resemble rubber gloves, since the entire arm and hand is molded from one piece of latex. They feel like real baby skin and the soft filling in the bodies make them very life-like.

Sun Rubber Company produced many dolls of both rubber and latex. The first Gerber Baby was produced by this company in all rubber in 1956. They also produced the latex Tod-L-Dee and Tod-L-Tim, two one-piece latex dolls with squeakers in the back and stationary eyes, with molded on clothing. These dolls are still quite easy to find at a few dollars each. A black Tod-L-Tim was seen at a doll show recently for $2.00 (with broken finger).

The first baby Tiny Tears with hard plastic head and molded hair, came assembled with a rubber body. (Did you know this doll must be rocked to sleep?) The Tiny Tears babies, because of their beautiful molding, are becoming more precious each year. Recently this first baby was seen for twenty-five dollars, although some can still be found for five to eight dollars.

Many well-known doll companies produced dolls made of latex. Of these, Cameo's Plum, Ideal's Tickletoes and Egee's Grace can still be found with a little searching. Vinyl was introduced and again we find a combination of materials. You may find a latex body with a vinyl head, for instance.

Three celluloid dolls from 1920s and 30s. Left to right: 5" celluloid bride, one piece with movable arms, original dress. Mark: Butterfly, Japan. $2 at doll show. 3½" celluloid, one piece body, movable arms, marked Occupied Japan. $2 at doll shop. 5½" black celluloid, jointed arms and legs, black fuzzy hair, yellow eyes. Marks 355¾ Empire made, $2.
Courtesy of Norma Quinn

Celluloid 9" clown including wheel from the 1940s. Wire arms, no legs, felt hands, high-wire rider. Flea market price $4, bargained down to $2. Mark on wheel: Made Germany/Western.

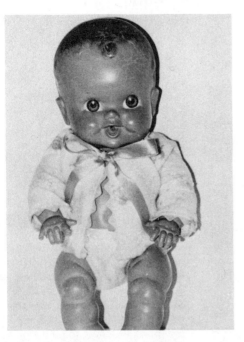

9" rubber "Amosandra," the baby of Amos 'n' Andy radio show fame. Orange stationary eyes, nurser mouth, dark brown molded hair. Marked "Amosandra," Columbia Broadcasting Inc., on head. Designed by Ruth Newton, manufactured by Sun Rubber Co. on back.

13" doll, 1940s. Stuffed one-piece latex body, legs and arms; hard plastic head, blue sleep eyes, closed mouth. Found at garage sale for $3.00; value: $12.

8" celluloid doll from France. Marked "Savoie" on black taffeta apron (in gold lettering). Black velour headdress with gold rope strap, painted features. Marks: Eagle Head/France/175/3. Originally priced $10.00 inside flea market—bargained down to $6; doll book value: $18. *Roger Fremier photo*

5½" celluloid doll dressed in costume of German province of Heidelburg. Strung arms and legs, blonde wig, painted features. $1.00 at flea market.

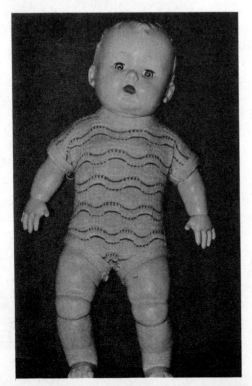

8" Mexican señor and señorita, 1940s.
All composition, original dress,
painted features, strung arms and
legs.
Courtesy of Lois Meade Harbert

9" composition Hollywood doll,
"Red Riding Hood." Molded shoes
and socks, glued-on blonde mohair
wig. Seen in varying costumes at
recent doll show for $3-$5, fair condition. *Courtesy of Patricia Smith
from E. Johnston collection*

10" Latex Tod-L-Dee and Tod-L-
Tim, 1953. Molded clothes, stationary eyes. $4 pair at flea market with
value of $8 pair. Manufactured by
Sun Rubber Co.

7" all-latex doll, 1940s. Stuffed body
and head, body and limbs one piece,
molded black hair, painted eyes
(paint has chipped off). No marks.
Flea market $1.

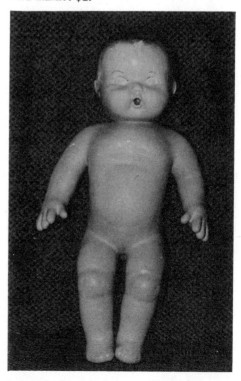

chapter 7

Stuffed Dolls

5½" doll from Panama. Dark beige floss-covered head; arms and legs of brown paper tubing; black cotton headdress trimmed with red and black; yellow cotton top; green and blue plaid skirt; embroidered features; rag stuffed. Outside flea market $2.00.

How far need we go back to find the beginning of the beloved, floppy, lovable stuffed dolls? Perhaps large leaves soaking in the marshes of the Nile were plucked by early civilizations and fashioned into silent playmates for their children. Stuffed dolls have been used as burial companions, and witchcraft and sorcery rites, but today they have a much happier role of being a soft comfort and happy companion of children.

Animal furs and skins were used very early for stuffed dolls. Needles were hewn from animal bones. As man learned to domesticate the animals, homespun material became the common covering for stuffed toys. Cloth dolls could be created within the confines of the home and doll-making became a favorite pastime on cold winter evenings.

The American Indians all devised their own methods of creating dolls. Noted more for the fine beadwork on the buckskin rather than the doll form, many stuffed Indian dolls have been preserved in Indian museums. Perhaps to promote anonymity, the faces either had no features or only slight hints of eyes and mouth. Real hair was often braided and attached. The Blackfoot, Sioux, Crow, Apache, Cheyenne, and Mojave Indians fashioned dolls not only from buckskin, but from cornhusks, wood, gourds, bones, clay, and other available materials. Today, softly stuffed dolls created for the tourist trade are usually of cotton, dressed in velvet and homespun materials with just a hint of the fine beading that was once so painstakingly added to the dolls. Should such an elaborately beaded doll be found, don't expect it to be priced for the ordinary consumer.

Indian dolls were not always just for the amusement of the young. They were symbolic of the Indians' spiritual beliefs. As with the wood Kachinas, Indian dolls often carried messages to their people. There were fertility dolls, medicine dolls, burial dolls, good fortune dolls, dolls of friendship, marriage, and harvest. Dolls served similar purposes for the Japanese and African cultures where they have included fetishes, amulets, and idols in the form of what we now recognize as dolls.

By the mid-1800s, patents were being applied for and the commercial rag doll became a promising business venture. In 1873 Izannah Walker, who had been making dolls for twenty years, received a patent for the rag dolls with round painted faces, and sateen heads reinforced with the expert use of paste to make them more resilient.

Martha Chase, residing, like Walker, in Rhode Island, was sufficiently inspired by the Walker rag dolls in those days of her youth to fashion a round-faced cotton-stuffed stockinette doll of her own. Martha's dolls began as toys for her family and friends, but soon became so popular that by 1895 the Chase rag dolls were being produced commercially. However, this was not the end of the Chase rag doll story. Today, Chase dolls, scaled to the correct proportions of human children and adults, are made specifically for use by hospital personnel in training classes.

It was inevitable that do-it-yourselfers would enter the stuffed doll market, much to the delight of premium collectors. Printed on sheets of cotton, the front and the back of a doll need only be cut out, sewn together and stuffed with any soft material found around the house. Many will remember Aunt Jemima of pancake flour fame; the Quaker Puffed Wheat hero, Puffy; Rastus from Cream of Wheat; and the Sunny Jim breakfast cereal cut-out. There are also cartoon characters such as Little Orphan Annie, Popeye, and Snoopy, the famous beagle created by Charles Schultz.

While wandering through a junk/antique store in a small California town in the summer of 1977, a small stuffed figure was seen lying in a crowded box with other goodies. It was a rather dingy looking 7½-inch figure with spindly legs and a chubby tummy. While I was holding the doll and still puzzling over it, the shop owner said, "That is a Brownie doll." When asked the price she said without even the slightest quiver in her voice, sixty-five dollars. My lips wouldn't even pucker to form a low whistle (which is my usual reaction to a too-high price). Seeing the look of amazement on my face, she said, "You'll never find another one like it." Rushing to my research books, I soon found that the Brownie is indeed quite rare, these little dolls being copyrighted in 1892 by Palmer Fox. When the Brownie camera came on the market in 1900, pictures of the

4" doll from Alaska. Leather head and body, sealskin suit, rabbit fur head and neckdress, felt hands and feet, painted features. $2 at outside show.

11" stuffed cotton doll, early 1960s, quite possibly done by a doll artist. Pressed felt face, mohair wig, white cotton dress with gold zig-zag trim. Given to author as gift.

7" all-leather Russian 1950s doll, carrying wood rifle. No marks. Collectible shop $14.

7" Panamanian worker 1965. Straw-stuffed cloth body and limbs, reinforced with wire; homespun cotton clothes with fringe trim. $1.50 inside flea market; value, $4.00.
Photo by Roger Fremier

Brownie figures could be seen on the simple cardboard boxes. These premium dolls by the Kodak Company are rather frog-like and charming, a good stuffed doll to look for, but don't be surprised at the price.

When John Gruelle was issued a patent in 1915 for Raggedy Ann, he began an American tradition. His Raggedy Ann and Raggedy Andy have endured through all these years to become a basic part of our Americana. Many similar designs have been made of the raggedy dolls, but the "doll with the heart that says 'I love you' is one of a kind."

Germany's most notable contribution to the stuffed doll era was performed by Kathe Druse, mother of seven children and wife of a successful German sculptor. The Kruse dolls of 1910 were among the first stuffed dolls to have the contour of the doll head sculped into likenesses of real children. Her nettle-cloth children were the product of much talent and imagination, emerging from her first experiments with potatoes and sand-filled cloth in an attempt to design a doll that looked and felt like a real person. She took the stuffed doll out of the realm of fanciful and comical characters and fashioned it into a non-smiling, life-like young child. The first dolls, stuffed with reindeer hair, had stiffened heads charmingly painted by hand in oil and the bodies of both the children and babies are chubby. World War II interrupted the import of these dolls, but the Kruse dolls survived to retain their popularity with Americans. The Rheinesche Gummi Und Celluloid Fabrik Company produced the Kruse dolls in plastic after the war. Kathe Kruse died in 1969, but her children continued the business and so the world is still blessed with Kathe Kruse dolls. (Doll Show price of a Kathe Kruse doll with the tag marking: Original Kathe Kruse Modell/ Hanne Kruse/was priced at $145. It was approximately 12 inches, stuffed arms, blonde wig.)

Another artist who began making replicas of unsmiling children was Sasha Morgenthaler of Switzerland. The most interesting aspect of the dolls which are called Sasha dolls is that through Mrs. Morgenthaler's love for children her dolls were born. During World War II, Sasha and her artist husband, Ernst, helped many people torn by the miseries of war to reach the Western Zone. The sad faces of the French and Italian children inspired Sasha to model the doll faces as we see them today. She has permitted 3 models of the Sasha dolls to be reproduced in plastic. They are Sasha, a sixteen-inch blonde girl, Gregory, a sixteen-inch brunette boy, and the baby Sasha, a twelve-inch doll who comes complete with a baby basket. The clothing on these dolls is not unusual; extra outfits can be purchased at the doll and toy store. The large dolls are $22.00, the baby $18.50. One glance at a Sasha doll tells you that it was modeled by a talented artist.

The peach-felt dolls of Madame Lenci produced in the 1920s are the work of another very talented artist. From this Italian factory came pouty-faced dolls of excellent taste not only in the modeling, but in the clothing that adorned them. A Lenci is another doll that is recognizable at first glance. There are two types of Lenci dolls. The first dolls were quite expensive and in order to bring the dolls within reach of the average persons they were made with cloth bodies and costumes which were not as elaborate. The Lenci dolls were made in all sizes, but the nine-inch felt dolls would fit well into a doll collection of smaller dolls.

Many of the Russian dolls have found their way into the hands of American collectors, often fashioned as tea cosies. The skirt of a tea cosy doll,

7" Raggedy Ann and Andy, 1976. Huggers sewn together at hands. Knickerbocker Toy Co. Garage sale 50 cents.

Contemporary 7½" cloth-stuffed Indian dolls. All hand stitched. No marks.
Courtesy of Lois Meade Harbert

1976 Navajo Indian woman grinding corn on rocks while bundled papoose sleeps nearby. Cloth-stuffed body, mohair wig, dark green velvet top, rayon skirt, yarn belt, small beaded earrings and necklace, painted features. Tiny cardboard basket contains four kernels of corn. Mounted on fiberboard, $6.00.

This 9" stuffed doll with stiffened brown felt head and black fur-type hair is a Jaku doll from West Germany and was originally dressed as Santa Claus in red cotton suit. However, when found at garage sale in 1960s, the suit was torn beyond repair. This new furry suit with brown suede mitts and boots seems to fit him well. Stuffed body, legs, and arms; painted black eyes, red dots at nostrils, and painted lips. Garage sale price, 25 cents; value, $15.00.

9" Russian tea cozy. Stockinette painted face, all cotton, believed to be World War I era. Flea market $5. *Courtesy of Norma Quinn*

usually quilted and stuffed with a soft filling, covering the fact that the dolls are legless. The skirt, as the name implies, covered a tea pot and kept the brew warm for expected visitors. The author found a rather large Russian tea cosy, dated around World War I, at a garage sale. It had been a present from a father to his young daughter while he served in the American Army. This doll has a papier-mâché painted head and is garbed in a soldier-like grey flannel coat and black trimmed hat.

The American adaptation of the tea cosy is of course the legless toaster cover dolls.

For the small doll collector, miniature versions of stuffed dolls, such as Raggedy Ann and Andy are quite easy to find today. However, in order to maintain a varied collection of small stuffed dolls, often we must be content to pursue dolls that are only partially made of cloth. Some of these small dolls are very charming and although they may have a mask composition, or papier-mâché faces and reinforced wire arms and legs, they nevertheless fit the cloth doll category.

One of the most charming of these small dolls that can still be found today are the Norah Wellings dolls that were manufactured in the Victoria Toy Works, Wellington, Shropshire, England from 1926-40s. World War II played an important part in Norah Wellings life and inspired her to create the now famous Sailor Boys and the parachutist named "Harry the Hawk" which she designed for the Royal Air Force. Also to her credit are Royal Canadians, Scots, and Black Islanders. One of her Darkies was seen at a doll show priced at thirty dollars, which seems quite expensive. Other Norah Wellings dolls are around fifteen dollars but can be bargained down to a more reasonable eight to ten dollars. Once you have seen a Norah Wellings doll, you will recognize all the other models she created. The Sailor Boy in his velvet navy outfit has been seen both with composition-type face and pressed felt face. Other war-time models created by this artist are nurses from the Red Cross, British soldiers and aviators. Because there have been many duplications of this doll because of its character face, it is wise to check for the Norah Wellings tag before purchasing it.

Rivaling the popularity of Raggedy Ann and promising as much happiness to each owner is our modern Holly Hobbie and her playmates, Heather and Carrie. Although Holly started out as a nostalgic bonnet girl on greeting cards in 1966, she soon became the star of hundreds of items, including desk sets, plates, stationary, clothing, etc. The first Holly doll was made in 1974. Both the entire stuffed doll form and the doll with the plastic face appeared in grand style on toy shelves all over America. There were, of course, accessories to accompany the dolls, including doll beds, sewing machines, watering cans, and a host of other items. Holly is dressed in a patchwork cotton dress with a blue bonnet decorated with tiny yellow flowers, and matching pantaloons. She has blonde yarn braids, white stuffed cotton legs with movable black straps glued to the black stuffed feet. Her dress tag reads: "The original HOLLY HOBBIE/Copyright American Greetings Corporation/All new materials Cotton & Synthetic Fibers/Surface washable only" and on the other side of the tag: "KTC emblem, Knickerbocker Toy Co. Inc./Middlesex, N.Y. 08848 USA/Made in Taiwan, Republic of China." There is a Department of Labor and Industry emblem in the center. Recently, the baby Holly appeared on the toy shelf, but alas, as adorable as she might be she is too large for the small doll collector.

Holly Hobbie is the real name of its American born creator, Denise Holly Hobbie, a talented artist born in 1944. Just as Rose O'Neill's Kewpies grew from sketches to dolls to a whole world of implike

8½" Lenci boy, 1921-1930s, as seen at doll show. There are two types of Lenci dolls. The first type brought to U.S. in the 1920s were all felt, elaborately dressed. These dolls were too expensive for the public market, so some later cloth-bodied Lencis were produced with less exquisite costumes. *Courtesy of Rhoda Shoemaker*

7" and 8" dolls, 1940s. Stuffed bodies and limbs, pressed paper heads, painted features, arms flesh-colored; boy has felt wig, girl mohair wig. Girl is carrying blue felt flowers. Boy has blue and white sailor outfit with white sailor hat, all felt. Stamped "Made in Italy" on shoes. Garage sale, $2.50.

8" Holly Hobbie and friend, Heather. All cotton with painted features. Found for 25 cents at garage sale; retails for $2.29.

lovables, so have Holly and her friends.

Fortunately, the wide spectrum of stuffed dolls has made it possible for many artists, both novice and professional, to create dolls of unlimited joy to children and collectors alike.

One contemporary doll artist, Jody Mehaffie creates Jody M. dolls which she designed and copyrighted. She has researched children's costumes from the Victorian era and dresses her fine handdyed muslin and kapok dolls in authentic laces and eyelets. This year she is exclusively making the Jody M. doll, called Victoria, and the list price is sixty-five dollars. Jody has assigned some of her dolls to Cottage Industies for production.

5½" Norwegian doll, 1965. All handmade, hand woven costume, leather-type shoes, felt hands, embroidered features. 50 cents flea market; value $8.00.

7" doll marked "Rosy" on red plastic shoes. Stuffed body and legs, plastic arms, mask face, red felt skirt with gold trim. Made in Italy. Garage sale 25 cents.

3" Chinese burial dolls, 1920s.
Stucco head, body, legs; stuffed
body. Male has one braid, female
has two braids. Buried with children.
Antique shop $3.00 each.

6¾" Norah Wellings doll. Suit is
navy blue velour. He has lost his
white English sailor hat. $4 inside
doll shop. *Courtesy of Norma Quinn*

11" stuffed "Mrs. Beasley." Painted
glasses and features, all cotton.
Buffie's doll on TV's "Family Affair."
The unfortunate death of this young
actress, Annisa Jones, has made Mrs.
Beasley even more dear to us. Found
for 25 cents at garage sale; retails
for $2.29.

Holly Hobbie cutout pattern dolls.
$1 per yard.

chapter 8

Storybook and
Costume Dolls

7" Ginny Doll by Vogue. All original, red felt hat tied with yellow ribbon, blue, red and white flannel shirt, leatherette skirt and weskit, red shoes, small metal gun at waist on green belt. Found by author for 50 cents at rummage sale; value, $15-$20.

For the collector who would like to collect small fine quality dolls without investing large sums of money, the storybook and costume dolls are a delightful place to start. One of the most satisfying features of collecting small dolls is that these can be displayed in an appealing manner without taking up a great deal of space. A small shelf cabinet, preferably glass enclosed will do nicely.

If you have obtained your small storybook and costume dolls at a bargain price, it doesn't seem to make sense to pay over a dollar for a stand. Therefore to be really conservative, you can place the dolls with the long skirts in a small jelly or juice glass. Since the skirt will hide the glass and still hold the doll securely, this makes a safe and inexpensive holder for your dolls.

NANCY ANN STORYBOOK

The Nancy Ann Storybook dolls in the painted bisque and hard plastic are highly collectible today. These storybook dolls have been a cheery addition to the doll world since 1941 when Nancy Ann Abbot began her small factory in California. What started out as a modest venture soon blossomed into a busy and profitable business.

Bisque
Up until the early 1950s, these storybook dolls were made of a slightly coarse bisque (especially noticeable on the arms and legs). The bisque is painted with a darker-than-flesh tone. Of all the Nancy Ann Storybook dolls, these are the most desirable today, since they are the oldest. There are several distinguishing features of the bisque storybook dolls: all the facial features are painted; the whites of the eyes have a slight blue tinge; black pupilless eyes, with upper-lashes hand painted show five to six lashes per eye in a gray tone; this gray color also outlines the upper eye; the mouth is a dab of oval red; there is a slight blush to the cheeks. With the adorable bumps for nostrils and the eyes tilting slightly upward, the entire face of this little doll has a shy and demure expression. The early bisques have body, legs, and head in one piece with movable arms. Later models also have movable legs. A rather rare, socket-head bisque is shown in il-

lustration. (Several of these were seen for six dollars at an outdoor flea market/antique show recently.) The mohair wigs on the Nancy Ann Storybooks are blonde, strawberry blonde and dark brown. If you have ever found one missing a wig, you will find a hole on top of the head.

These dolls came boxed in red, pink, and blue polka-dot boxes. Inside the box was a pamphlet naming the different series of storybooks available. On the wrist of the doll was a gold tag, giving the name of the doll on one side and "Storybook Dolls by Nancy Ann" on the other side. According to the two different pamphlets that have been found in the original boxes of these storybook dolls of bisque, the following series of dolls were available: Fairytale Series, Bridal Series, Seasons Series, Dolls of the Days, Undressed Series, Dolls of the Month Series, Powder and Crinoline Series, and the three series which were originally called simply the "Storybook Series"—Mother Goose series, Fairyland Series, and Nursery Rhyme Series.

If any doll needs to be dressed in its original costume it is the Nancy Ann Storybook doll, for without it, she is not truly a storybook doll. This does not mean that there is only *one* dress for each named character! As seen in illustration. Over the Hill was found with two ensembles, differing in both color and material, but matching in *style*. One collector has found as many as five different colored materials on a doll with the same name. Therefore, at best, all the collector can hope for is that the doll can

The many bodies of Nancy Ann Storybook Dolls. (Left to right) 6½" bisque socket head; 5½" bisque one-piece head and body, jointed arms; 5½" bisque with jointed legs and arms; 6½" painted hard plastic, one-piece head and body; 6½" painted hard plastic with jointed arms and legs, swivel head; light cream-tone plastic with jointed arms and legs, swivel head.

5½" bisque "Mistress Mary."
Courtesy of Lois Meade Harbert

be identified by the *style* given that particular named doll. It is easy to identify Red Riding Hood with the red cape, or Pocket-Full-Of-Posy with one flower in the pocket, or One-Two-Button-My-Shoe with the painted three-button shoe, but not all are so clearly distinguishable.

The underclothing is either short or long-legged in heavy to sheer cotton, plain or with lace. On the bisques, the dresses are fastened with a small gold pin in the back and the underclothing is also held closed with the same pin. The shoes are painted black and their ensembles are complimented with felt hats, ribbons, flowers, feathers, and various head coverings. Material for the clothing includes homespun to sheer cottons, taffetas, lace, etc.

There are variations in the markings of the bisque storybooks. The markings on the center back could be:

STORY	STORY	STORY	NANCY
BOOK	BOOK	BOOK	ANN
DOLL	DOLL	DOLL	STORYBOOK
U.S.A.	U.S.A.	U.S.A.	DOLL
	pat app for	11	

Some of the dolls have come through unmarked, or appear to be unmarked. Although a closer scrutiny may find the mold marks there, the letters did not successfully come out of the mold.

The Nancy Ann bisque Storybooks sold for $1.25. Also included in the box with some dolls was a stand for the doll, with plastic black base and green plastic holder. Inscribed on the base was *Nancy Ann Storybook Dolls*. Some of the dolls have been found with a red cardboard heart placed in a cut-out over

Three examples of "Dolls-of-Month" Nancy Ann Storybooks. (From left to right) Miss June — "A Rosebud Girl to Love Me Thru the June Days" No. 192; Miss November — "A November Lass to Cheer" No. 197; Miss May — "A Flower Girl for May" No. 191.

the top of the doll. Of course the most desirable Nancy Ann Storybook is one complete with box, wrist tag and original outfit. Fortunately, because they were small and could be tucked away, many of these bisques have come to us in like new condition. Prices vary from one area to another. Without box or tag, but in original clothes and good condition, the bisques are being sold at flea markets and doll shows for five to eight dollars. Boxed with all original accessories, they may be as high as fifteen to twenty dollars although bargains can still be found on these too.

Plastic
When Nancy Ann Storybook Doll Company began using hard plastic for their dolls, they continued with the same skin tone and painted features as the bisques. Therefore, it is nearly impossible to tell at a distance whether such a doll is bisque or hard plastic. They appear more similar to the 6½-inch bisques with longer necks and thinner faces. One collector stated she quickly identified them by trying to move the head (the plastic ones swivel), but this is not always true, since some of the early plastics have stationary heads! But the weight of the lighter plastic is obvious; the smoothness of the hard plastic is also obvious. If still in doubt, the clear printing of the markings on the back reveal the plastic surface: "STORYBOOK / DOLLS / U.S.A. / Trademark / Reg."

By 1947, Nancy Ann Storybook dolls of hard plastic were produced with a much lighter skin tone, rivaling the delicate look of wax. These plastic cream-toned dolls have sleep eyes (early ones black, later ones blue). They are dressed in similar ensembles and the clothing is held by a snap and the under pantaloons secured with tape. There are also teen sisters and a baby in plastic. These dolls can still be found as real bargains—as low as 50 cents and usually not higher than $3 in excellent condition. The darker-toned plastics may be higher, possibly $4—$5 in the original box.

In 1970, the vinyl Nancy Ann's were produced. Few of these are yet seen on the bargain tables. Once they have aged a little, it is certain they, too, will be snatched up by collectors who will help to perpetuate the name of Nancy Ann Abbott.

Two versions of "A Shower Girl for April": one in bisque, one in dark plastic. (Left) 6½" bisque; peach dress with lace and blue trim, blue felt hat with blue flowers tied with darker peach ribbon, white lace umbrella with pipe-stem handle wound around wrist, dark blonde. (Right) Painted dark-tone plastic, dressed in yellow with flocked white flowers on dress, felt hat with white flower, darker yellow rayon umbrella, pipe-stem handle. Original price for bisque was $10, bargained down to $5 with purchase of several dolls; plastic doll $4 at doll show.

Two versions of Nancy Ann Bridesmaid. (Left) Light plastic, peach-pink dress with white lace, matching lace and ribbon headdress, pink flowers. (Right) 5½" bisque, light lavender dress with ecru lace and trim, headdress of lace with pink ribbon, pink flower at waist with streamer of pink ribbon, brunette. No. 87 bridesmaid on wrist tag.

Nancy Ann Storybook dolls. (Left) Bisque "Little Red Riding Hood" with plastic cape and white dress, near her red polka dot box. (Right) "One, Two, Button My Shoe," with painted three-button shoes. Shown in her original red heart cutout in red polka dot box. Flea market price, $5.00; doll show price, $10; doll book price, $12-$15.

Two versions of the 5½" Nancy Ann Storybook doll called "Over the Hills" No. 114. (Left) Blue felt hat with blue ribbon, pink cotton dress with blue trim, blonde. (Right) White felt hat with red ribbon, white dress with blue and red trim, and red flowers, brunette.

MADAME ALEXANDER

If doll collectors were ever forced to choose only one doll company from which to gather their flock of beautiful dolls, it is quite certain that many collectors would, without hesitation, shout "Madame Alexander". Madame Alexander dolls are dolls with class, never assembled hastily or without forethought; the exquisite costuming and the beautiful sculpted bodies and faces are the utmost in quality.

Fortunately for the small-doll collectors, there are adorable eight-inch dolls in hard plastic to add to their collections. Mothers gather Alexander dolls such as these to pass down to their children, and their children's children, with the hope that there will always be an Alexander doll in the family.

The Alexander Doll Company began in 1923 in New York with Madame Bertha Alexander as the founder. Madame Alexander came to the doll world with the best experience possible—her parents had operated a doll hospital in the United States beginning in 1895. From the parade of dolls that came into her parents' doll hospital, Madame Alexander obtained first hand a knowledge of beautiful old dolls, the stories that went with the dolls, the reconstruction of broken bodies, and the artistry of costuming.

The first Alexander dolls were made of cloth with three-dimensional facial features, and by the 1930s a series of seven-inch composition storybook dolls had come onto the market. Dolls such as Alice in Wonderland were the first to represent a philosophy behind the Madame Alexander dolls—a hope that the dolls will nurture in the child a feeling of understanding for others.

The eight-inch plastic Alexander dolls were created to represent storybook characters, dolls of other lands, star personalities, and nursery rhyme characters. In 1965, Madame Alexander International dolls representing each nation in the United Nations were on display at New York's City Hall and Madame Alexander was honored by Arthur Goldberg, United State Ambassador to the UN on United Nations Day, October 22. Madame Alexander dolls are exhibited in museums throughout the world, including a permanent exhibit at the Congressional Club, Washington, D.C. (dolls representing various cultures of the United States), and the Children's Trust Museum in New Delhi, India. In 1968, Madame Alexander dolls portraying the Revolutionary and Civil War eras were presented to the Smithsonian Institution in Washington D.C. Madame Alexander has earned a lifetime membership in the Brooklyn Institute of Arts and Sciences.

In the 1950s and 60s, the small Alexander dolls were walkers with bending knees in the eight-inch category. These dolls seem to be most highly prized and at some doll shows the asking price is thirty-five dollars!

Today, the eight-inch dolls are still available and include the International and Storyland Dolls. The superb craftmanship is still obvious in the dolls. Two hundred different materials go into the manufacture of a single doll and the many molding processes produce durable and beautiful dolls. The International Dolls (thirty-seven in all) are authentically dressed in their native costumes. They are meant to be a source of information and understanding of both customs and costumes of foreign lands. The Storyland Series include such favorite nursery rhyme characters as Little Bo-Peep, Hansel and Gretel, Miss Muffet, Red Riding Hood and Mary Mary (Quite Contrary). The characters in Louisa M. Alcott's book, *Little Women*, are immortalized in the Alexander dolls (see illustration), as are dolls such as Scarlett O'Hara, heroine of *Gone With the Wind*, depicting the Civil War era.

The beautiful eight-inch dolls of the Madame Alexander Company are now $13.95 and come in blue boxes with "Madame Alexander" printed in pink and green in a triangular design, with pink

7" Muffie, 1952, all hard plastic Nancy Ann Storybook. Clothes not original but of excellent design, blue sleep eyes, head turns as walks, dark brown wig. $5 at inside flea market.

8" Madame Alexander "Little Women" series in hard plastic. (Top row left to right) Beth, Laurie, Marmee, Meg. (Bottom row left to right) Amy, Jo. $13.95. *Courtesy of Madame Alexander Doll Company*

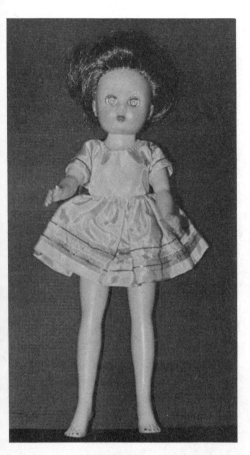

Nancy Ann hard vinyl, 1959. Jointed waist, high heel shoes, red-rooted hair, molded lashes. Mark: Nancy Ann on head. $1 at flea market; value $8.

flowers inserted in some of the triangles. The doll is wrapped in pink tissue paper and on the box it says "Alexander Doll Company, N.Y., N.Y." (More is said about Alexander dolls in chapter eleven.)

One fact is certain—Madame Alexander dolls will continue to be loved and admired by children and adults for all the years to come, and as a modern collectible doll, it is tops.

GINNY

I happened upon my first Ginny doll quite by accident in my early days of doll collecting. There it was on a rummage sale table, along with other dolls of various sizes. The tag said 50 cents. Although I had no idea what kind of doll it was, I recognized it as a well-made doll that had more than its share of charm. Later I was to learn that I had purchased the cowgirl Ginny in her original costume, complete down' to the tiny toy gun hanging from her waist. My 50 cent investment was worth fifteen to twenty dollars! Of course, the more I learned about the Ginny dolls, the less inclined I was to sell her.

In the 1930s, when our economic position was at its worst, Mrs. Jennie Graves had problems of her own. Left a widow with two young daughters to raise, she called upon her own talent of designing and sewing doll clothes. Her company, the Jordan Marsh Company of Boston, expanded in spite of it all, and friends and neighbors helped to make clothes for the dolls. Ginny began as a composition doll in the latter 1930s (now priced at $37.50 in a doll show). As her popularity grew, so did her wardrobe and her family. Mrs. Graves commissioned a German sculptor in 1948 to design what we now know as the 7—7½-inch hard plastic Ginny. The dolls had painted eyes and mohair wigs and were fully jointed. By 1951, Ginny had a complete wardrobe with matching accessories and furniture scaled to match her small stature. In the early 1950s, Ginny had progressed to sleep eyes. There were also Ginnys with dynel wigs, and for one year only, 1952, Ginny was designed with a lambs-wool poodle cut.

Mrs. Grave's daughter, Virginia Graves Carlson, for whom the doll was named was now designing all the little garments for the separately packaged Gin-

ny ensembles. In the next few years members of
Ginny's family were added, including 8-inch Baby
Ginnette with lambs-wool wig and bent baby legs;
10½-inch teenage sister Jill with jointed knees, high-
heels and an adult figure; 11½-inch Jeff, the big
brother or boyfriend; and Jan, who has been called
both a sister and a girlfriend of Jill's. By 1953 the
series of Ginny dolls included: Kindergarten Afternoon Series; Kindergarten School Series; Twin
Series; Tiny Miss Series; Gadabout Series; Fable
and Bride Series, and Debutante Series (6 dolls to a
series). By 1957, Ginny had walking knees. All
through the 1950s Ginny was the ultimate fashion
model. She had costumes from Far Away Lands,
outfits for Sun Time, Rain or Shine, bridal gowns
and many more. Ginny dolls had both blue and
brown eyes, but fewer of the brown eyes have been
found, making a brown-eyed Ginny more valuable
to the collector. In 1960, Mrs. Graves retired and
members of her family carried on. By this time Ginny had another brother, 8-inch Jimmy, with molded
hair and painted eyes.

By 1963, Ginny had been given a vinyl head and

8" Madame Alexander "Storyland" series
hard plastic dolls. (Top row left to right)
Bride, Red Boy. (Bottom row left to
right) Scarlett O'Hara, Ballerina,
Betsy Ross.

Two 5½" Hollywood dolls. (Left) Blue felt hat, blue cotton dress, both accented with dark pink ribbon, dress trim dark blue polka dots on white, brown mohair wig, swivel head. (Right) Halloween doll in orange and black, pipe-stem broom with multi-color yarn, black felt hat with black trim. Can be found for less than $6 list price.

"Ginny" dolls. (Front) Miss 1900, composition; Miss 1910, composition; Miss 1920, hard plastic with painted eyes. (Back) Miss 1930, hard plastic, painted eyes; Miss 1940, Miss 1950, Miss 1960, all hard plastic with sleep eyes.

in 1966 the whole doll was vinyl, thus ending the walking Ginny. In 1968, Ginny was no longer being produced in the United States, although Hong Kong reproductions from the 1966 molds were being produced in 1972.

Ginny, one of our first tiny toddlers, is an adorable doll. She has her own doll club and a book entitled *That Doll Ginny*, authored by the president of the doll club, Jeanne Niswonger, should now be available. The price of Ginnys has risen sharply and many doll clothes experts have profited from making exquisite outfits for all the Ginny dolls that come to us unclothed. Ginny is durable and enchanting. She will be with us for a long time. As you come to know Ginny, you will be able to recognize her from the other copies that were made in her likeness. She is marked "Ginny" and/or "Vogue Doll." If you see her at a bargain for under five dollars, it is wise to add her to your collection now, for Ginny is becoming more precious to us all.

HOLLYWOOD DOLLS

When you find a small 5½-inch plastic doll with a star on its back, you will know that you are looking at a Hollywood Doll. These dolls began as the Ginnys, in composition with painted features and

mohair wigs, in the 1940s. They stood nine inches tall and their shoes and socks were molded and painted. Although some of these dolls were said to have been made in bisque, they simply are not seen today and the author pleads ignorance of this doll.

The founder of the Hollywood Dolls was Domenick Ippolite and for over a decade and a half his dolls were prolifically manufactured. The composition dolls are marked "Hollywood Doll" on the back, but the smaller plastic ones have the now well known star, with the words "Hollywood Doll" in raised letters on the back of the doll. In spite of their small size, the Hollywood dolls are dressed in enchanting detail, always with some type of head decoration topped with laces, flowers and ribbons. The plastic dolls have sleep eyes and movable legs.

They also came in several series, including Mother Goose, Nursery Rhymes, Toyland, Hollywood Lucky Stars, Days of the Week and many other characters such as Cowgirl, Sleeping Beauty, Little Miss Bunnie, and Bride. On the bargain table, a Hollywood doll is very seldom found in her original box, although I have seen her tied securely in place, with skirts spread out to show off her colorful clothes. If she is undressed when found, it will probably never be known who she had been. The Hollywood dolls fit in well with the other storybooks in a small collection. Top price for a plastic Hollywood seems to be running near six dollars, although composition ones have been seen for less. A doll in fair condition costs about two to three dollars and these little charmers are well worth the money.

DUCHESS DOLLS

Why do we know so little about Duchess Dolls? Even well informed collectors do not seem to have all the pertinent information about these dolls. It seems that they may be the "sleepers" of the small doll world, since their costumes are exquisite and well above the average costuming of other plastic dolls being found at rummage sales and flea markets. Most of the Duchess Dolls were made in 1948 or 1949, although the company is believed to have been in business until 1952. You may need a magnifying glass to be able to read the engraving on the back of

4" plastic Hollywood baby. All original, including box. $5.00.
Courtesy of Norma Quinn

7" Duchess "Tinker Bell," 1948. Hard plastic, blonde glued-on wig, paper wings trimmed with gold, green velour suit, molded shoes. $7.00 value.
Courtesy of Lois Meade Harbert

the doll, but it will read "Duchess Doll Corp/Design Copyright"/year. The Duchess Dolls are of a shiny plastic with molded white shoes. They have glued on mohair wigs, their body and legs in one piece, and their arms and head jointed. The 1947 Duchess Doll has painted eyes. They range in size from 7–7½ inches. The Duchess Doll Groom is very interesting. He has painted black hair and shoes; comes with both painted and sleep eyes; is dressed in grey striped felt pants, black felt long-tailed tuxedo and black felt hat, both trimmed with black ribbon. He has a pearl tie and a simulated carnation in his lapel.

Some of the best known Duchess Dolls are Tinker Bell and Peter Pan, manufactured in 1948. Also well-known are such celebrities as Miss Holland, Carmen, Martha Washington, Miss North America, and Miss Tastee Freez, to name a few. Unfortunately, the clothes are usually stapled onto the doll (which makes doll collectors cringe). However, their costumes alone are well worth the average selling price of two to five dollars.

8" Internationals from Madame Alexander Co. (Top, left to right) Indonesia, Portugal, Turkey. (Bottom left to right) Rumania, Yugoslavia, Norway. $13.95 each.

Duchess groom, 1949. Painted hair, sleep eyes. Duchess doll on right dressed in lovely pink satin dress trimmed with ecru lace, strawberry-blonde mohair wig, blue sleep eyes. $1 at rummage sale; $5-$8 value each.

NATIONAL COSTUMES

Dolls in costumes of their homeland are very appealing and collected by many. Some are much better made than others, with authentic clothing down to the most minute detail. It can be confusing to find a doll, for instance, made in Germany that has an English costume. Sometimes the name of the country is not noted, and it is the collector's guess as to exactly what nation it is supposed to represent. Madame Alexander dolls, as mentioned, have received worldwide recognition for their authentic costuming from other nations. Some of the dolls in national dress are included in other chapters because of their construction. The stuffed doll (see illustration) was especially exciting to find, since careful scrutinizing revealed the fact that its dress was hand-woven material. This doll was pictured among fine authentic dolls in a January 1965 issue of *Woman's Day*. As jet travel gives us the opportunity to reach other countries in a matter of hours, closer understanding between all cultures should be nurtured. While watching a Sunday evening program of Wild Kingdom and beautiful film of the Laplander people, I realized that one of the dolls I had picked up at a flea market was dressed exactly as the people in the film. "That's my doll" I heard myself saying. Through our dolls we can retain the admiration and respect we have for the diverse and interesting cultures of the world.

7-7½" Duchess doll in Dutch costume, 1949. Yellow felt hat, white felt gown top, yellow skirt with blue felt trim, blue sleep eyes, blonde mohair wig. $2.50 at flea market; $5-$6 value.

7" soft vinyl. Rabbit fur and feather decoration. Found in unmarked red box at garage sale for 25 cents.

5" dancer with clay head and hands. Stuffed legs and body, painted black boots, felt skirt and weskit, floss hair. Wire in right shoe to hold it on stand. Found at thrift shop for $3.50.

1976 Bicentennial doll, all plastic, 8". Mark on box: Manufactured in Hong Kong for EK S.S. Kresge Co. Troy, Michigan. Mark on doll: Made in Hong Kong. Reddish-blonde rooted hair, blue sleep eyes. White felt hat, gray cotton dress, white apron, white cotton stockings, removable white plastic shoes. Retail price: $3.00.

7" dancing girl with wind-up key in back. Celluloid-type plastic with painted head, painted shoes and socks. All one piece except strung arms, black felt hat. Found for $2 at flea market, $8 value.

The Fashions Of 1776

Ultra deluxe satin gown on this 7" Duchess doll, 1949. Pale lavender gown with pink satin ribbon, floss pink flowers and green leaves, blue flower at waist, blue felt hat, strawberry-blonde mohair wig. Given to author as gift; value, $6-$7.

6" authentically dressed celluloid Laplander, 1960s. Heavy cotton blue leggings trimmed with red felt, leather boots with turned-up toes, red yarn bound ankles. Molded hair (no color), blue sleep eyes, strung arms and legs. Made in Italy. Flea market price 75 cents; value, $4.00.

3½" German plastic with strung arms and legs, blonde, braided wig. Green felt hat with white feather, red cotton dress, white apron trimmed with black felt, painted shoes and socks. Good detail for such a small doll. Found for 50 cents at garage sale; value, $3.50.

9" Chinese baby with stucco head, limbs, and arms. Stuffed body, black wig, stationary inset glass eyes. $4 in doll shop.
Courtesy of Norma Quinn

chapter 9

Plastic
and
Vinyl Dolls

3" plastic Red Riding Hood, 1960s. Red felt hood, red and white cotton checkered skirt, sleep eyes. Received free from seller after purchasing several dolls. Tag on skirt: Made in Italy. Chair sculptured from aluminum can, red velvet seat. $4.00 value.

All of the different types of plastic and vinyl dolls manufactured over the past twenty-five to thirty-five years are too voluminous to be included in one chapter of this book. Since the storybook and costume dolls were discussed in a chapter of their own, it was decided to select some of the more unusual vinyl and plastic dolls of the 1940s and 50s and the ones that just happened to come along during my travels through the marts. Most of the dolls in these years, because of the competitiveness in the doll industry, had a gimmick to attract the attention of the children. There were dolls with hair that grew; dolls with adult figures; dolls with foreign playmates; wind-up dolls; dolls with houses and extensive wardrobes; and of course there were the magnificently ugly, but lovable trolls. Television advertisements helped to increase sales, as any young mother will attest to.

If you are a beginning collector, collecting the modern dolls is a good place to start. You can make all your mistakes on the less expensive dolls and by the time you are ready to buy a fine, valuable old doll, you will be a seasoned and shrewd buyer.

You will have many choices when selecting modern dolls. In spite of all the rules that could be set down on what to buy and what not to buy, it all boils down to one important fact: if you like the doll—if it really does something to you—then buy it. The most important thing is that the doll bring real pleasure to you. This is especially true if you plan to keep the doll. If you are buying with the idea of selling or trading the doll, that is a different matter which we shall discuss later.

Of course, I do not advocate paying the first price that is offered—especially at flea markets and junk shops, no matter how much you like the doll. (You can always pay full price if all else fails.) When you first start to bargain on a price, you will feel a little embarrassed, but once you find it *works*, you will be braver the next time! Actually, bargaining for a good price can be lots of fun for everyone. It's sort of a game we all play, with the doll as the big prize.

There are several ways to bargain. One of the easiest ways is to simply ask:"What is your bottom price on this?" Usually the seller will come down slightly with this approach. However, it seems to work more to your advantage to make the bargaining more of a challenge—a little spicier. Let us say you have seen a doll for eight dollars. You might offer the ridiculously low price of two dollars. The seller may shake his/her head and probably say "I couldn't take less than six." You then act as though this is a horribly high price, mull the doll over in your hands, point out the flaws (don't get too carried away with finding fault with the doll or the seller may become insulted), then give some further reason for not wanting to pay the price, such as "I really don't need this particular doll," or "I just can't afford to spend that much money today," or have a friend standing nearby who reminds you at the most critical moment that you must save enough money for lunch. Meanwhile the seller has been standing by listening to your mutterings. Now is the time to make another offer. You have gotten the seller down from eight dollars to six. You have offered two. You might then offer four dollars. Sometimes at this point the seller will take it; other times the seller will "split the difference" and come down to five dollars. You have then saved yourself three dollars on an eight dollar doll, which is not bad for a beginning.

Some flea market shoppers will offer one low price and stick to it (usually on a doll he/she could do without anyway). The seller may keep offering a little less and then either let you have it for the cheap price or just stop bargaining. Another good way to get the price down is to leave the doll and start to walk away. Sometimes the seller will call you back and say "OK, two dollars!" Or, when you come back around to that table later (if the doll isn't sold by then) you can make another offer. If it is getting quite late in the day and the doll hasn't been sold, usually your offer will be accepted.

If the seller has many articles on a table and you see one doll you would really like but the price is too high, take an interest in something else on the table that doesn't especially appeal to you. Ask the price and then immediately set it down as though it is much too expensive. You might do this a few times to convince the seller you are not willing to pay the prices that are marked. Then go to the doll you really want and ask the price. Usually the seller will say, "Well, you can have that for three dollars (or what-

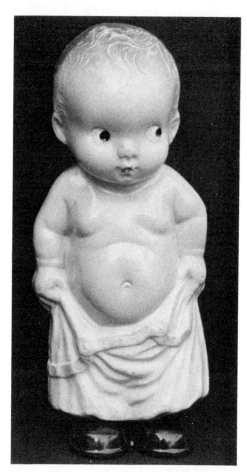

6½" wind-up boy, 1950s, of plastic. Molded one piece except for moving feet. Molded brown hair, side-glancing eyes painted black with blue, blue molded playsuit. Mark on back in circle: Irwin, Made in U.S.A. At doll show for $20; flea market price $3.

9" Cissette bride by Madame Alexander Doll Co., 1957. Walker knees jointed. $4.00 garage sale, value $15-$20. *Courtesy of Lois Meade Harbert*

8" Miss Chicadee, 1948, by American Character Doll Company. All original, hard plastic, molded hair, painted features. *Courtesy of Patricia Smith*

ever)," which is much less than the original asking price.

When looking for the modern dolls you will sometimes have to decide whether or not you are going to buy a doll without its original clothing. Since many of the modern dolls are not too old, chances are you will be able to find one with its original clothes if you hold out for it. An all-original doll in mint condition is more valuable for resale. However, this is not to say that beautiful clothes cannot make the doll just as charming. Often duplicates of the original clothes can be made for very little money, which is why many sewers are always on the look-out for old laces and cloth to make clothing.

There are three things that will reduce the price of a doll immediately—ill-fitting clothes; damaged or broken dolls; or just plain dirty, messed up dolls. The dolls can be redressed and cleaned up, but a doll that is damaged is going to lose it's value very quickly.

I cannot emphasize enough how important it is to learn about dolls through doll books. You will learn the approximate value of the dolls, the age of the dolls, what the original outfits were, and what marks to look for to identify the dolls. The modern doll collector books are invaluable in helping to educate yourself about the doll market. In the beginning, at least, you might take the doll book with you (you can then quickly go back to the car and make a check when you are in doubt). As you become better informed, you will be able to recognize the approximate age of the doll by the material from which it is made, and will also have many of the facts memorized from the books.

Sometimes to put a doll back in shape, you will have to search for missing parts. I have paid $2.50 for an undesirable doll just because I recognized the dress as belonging to another doll. In this case it was the orange lace dress that belonged to Beautiful Crissy, but the seller had put it on another doll of comparable size. Sometimes the seller will let you have the dress for a small price, but usually they will not, since doll clothes are hard to find. One collector who was selling her collection gave me the body for the lovely hard plastic Bonnie Walker (I recognized the number on the back of the doll) but the head was missing. When I walked into a doll show a few months later, there was the head, in beautiful condition, for 50¢! I then had a lovely hard plastic doll from the 1950s for a mere half-dollar. In another instance, I had picked up a vinyl-headed Betsy McCall for 25¢ at a flea market, but the face was badly smeared with felt pen, which no amount of sunshine, or oil, or lemon juice, or anything else would take out. I asked this same collector if she by chance had a Betsy McCall head, which she did. I bought it for $1. For $1.25 I then had a very nice $15 doll. However, beware of persons who put parts on dolls that do not really belong to them! Many of the original bodies of the first Tiny Tears dolls were rubber and badly deteriorated, although the hard plastic head remained in excellent condition. Often you will find replaced bodies on these dolls. The buyer should be notified if a doll part has been replaced before purchasing it, but this does not always happen and so it is up to you to carefully check the doll before your spend your money on it.

8" tiny Betsy McCall, American Character Doll Company. All original, hard plastic, skull cap rooted hair. Marks: McCall Corporation in circle on center of back. 1958. If not dressed, can be found at flea markets for $4-$6; original value, $17-$20.

As you search for dolls from the last three decades, such well-known doll companies as Alexander Doll Company, American Character, Arranbee, Cameo, DeLuxe Reading, Ideal, Mattel, Remco, Sun Rubber, Terri Lee, Egee (E.G. Goldberger), Horsman, Uneeda, Vogue, Walt Disney (R. Dakin), and Knickerbocker will become familiar to you.

Among the small dolls that you may find manufactured by Alexander Doll Company (from 1923 to the present) might be the Storybook, International and Storyland dolls; the nine-inch Cissettes; Little Genius—a seven-inch vinyl doll with a hard plastic head from 1958 (which is now worth twenty dollars); and the vinyl ten-inch Little Shaver of 1963, to name a few.

American Character Doll Company (1918-1960s) manufactured the eight-inch Miss Chicadee, Teensy Betsy McCall (look for a small circle in center of the back marked "McCall Corp"), and the New Tiny Tears manufactured in 1964 that came in all sizes, and whose right hand holds a pacifier.

Arranbee (R&B) (1922-1959, named used to 1960) is well known for its Littlest Angel dolls in the small hard plastic.

Cameo (began 1922—sold to Strombecker in 1970) of course brings us Kewpies, in vinyl too.

Adorable 5" vinyl "Kim," 1970, with growing blonde hair, red beauty mark on lower left cheek, blue eye shadow, painted black eyes. Dark blue suede cloth dress with pearl buttons, light blue removable shoes. Uneeda (marked UD Co.) Made in Hong Kong. Value in doll shops, $3-$4. *Photo by Roger Fremier*

Two of the small DeLuxe Reading dolls that can still be found quite easily are eight-inch Penny Brite from the 1960s and seven-inch Susie Cute, both in vinyl.

Effanbee (F&B, 1910 to the present) produced small dolls such as Pumpkin and Half Pint who are well worth searching for.

Horsman (1860s to the present) always has adorable dolls that are almost instantly recognizable, some of the most well-liked being the early vinyl dolls that look almost like wax, the coloring becomes more beautiful as it ages and turns darker.

Ideal (1902 to the present) is well known for many dolls, but their newborn and minute Thumbelinas are unusual and irresistible, as are their Flatsie dolls from the 1960s.

Mattel (1945 to the present) captured the hearts of all of us with their Little Kiddles that were a mere three inches or less, had their own beds and accessories, could be worn as lockets and charms. They also had many adorable comic characters such as the Charlie Brown gang, Dr. Doolittle, and the Barbie family.

Remco brought us Heidi and Jan, the two 5½-inch friends from different countries, and Sweet April, a 5½-inch all-vinyl doll that moves its arms and cries.

The Terri Lee Company (1948-1955) began by producing some early composition dolls, but is better known for its all hard plastic dolls of the 1950s that have an almost waxlike appearance. The tiny Baby Linda doll by Terri Lee is very collectible and this all-vinyl baby is selling for twenty to thirty-five dollars in doll shows.

Uneeda Doll Company (1917 to the present) has made dolls of all types, including teenagers, babies that love to bathe, beautiful walking dolls, tiny Kim with hair that grows, and character dolls such as Penelope and her six sisters.

Vogue (1930s) of course brought us Ginny and her family, a Littlest Angel and many others.

Walt Disney (R. Dakin), enriched our lives with Disney character dolls such as snow White and the Seven Dwarfs, the Mickey Mouse family, Donald Duck, and all those happy characters we watched with such glee in the cartoons.

There are also some lovely dolls of foreign manufacture that you will find and like very much. The Furga and Italo-cremora dolls of Italy are always magnificently dressed and very well made; also the Italian dolls marked Ratti; in France, Jumeau produced some composition plastics in the 1950s and there are some beautiful waxlike dolls with muted features by C.R. Club from France in the stores today. England has provided us with the Nesbit dolls, seen both in composition and plastic, with tags on their arms. Germany's Rheinische Gummi Und Celluloid Fabrik Company also manufactured some very nice plastic dolls when celluloid was discontinued.

These are only a sampling of the dolls you will find and each one you discover has its own unique charm.

Fortunately most of the plastic and vinyl dolls are marked with the company name on the back of the head or shoulder, and by the 1960s the year of manufacture was also included in the markings. If the doll is not marked, you may be lucky enough to find it with its original clothes, which may have an attached tag that will furnish the information you need to identify it (although this is not foolproof, since the clothes could be changed; however, usually the fit of the clothes will help you to tell if they are the originals). Your doll books will also be of tremendous help, but of course if you do not know the company of manufacture, you will have to leaf

Paper-dressed 6¾" native. Head, body, and legs in one piece. Yellow sleep eyes with molded lashes, molded shoes, black karacul wig. Marks: Made in England, on back. Garage sale 25 cents, value $6.00.
Photo by Roger Fremier

A group of Flatsy dolls, 1969, by Ideal. All vinyl, bendable for different poses. Doll on Flatsy horse has cowboy outfit. Small doll 2½", medium 5", tall 8½", $1-$3.

8" Penny Brite, 1963, by Deluxe Reading Co. Blonde rooted hair, original dress, all vinyl. Seen frequently at flea markets and doll shows for $4-$6.

through the books page by page until you find it. Both for insurance purposes and for your own recollection, complete records should be kept of your dolls—when they were purchased, their identification, the price paid for the doll, and if possible, a picture of the doll. Each doll can also be tagged as soon as you buy it, keeping this information tied around the wrist or pinned to the clothing. Any interesting stories connected with the doll should also be written down, since you may forget the details of the story as time passes.

When trying to identify a doll that is not marked, you might keep in mind the years that certain materials were used for dolls. You can closely pinpoint the date of manufacture, for instance, of the hard plastic dolls that date from the latter 1940s to 1960, although many companies began using vinyl heads (and sometimes limbs) on their hard plastic dolls by the mid 1950s. The early plastics of the 1940s look much like the composition that preceded them, both in coloring and molding. Vinyl began to be used in 1951 and many of these early dolls of the 1950s have stuffed one-piece bodies. The early thick vinyl ages into a mellow yellowish brown. The soft plastics appeared by the mid 1950s and of course since then the hard and soft vinyls and plastics have progressed to dolls of babylike softness. If a doll has a wig it can be dated approximately from the 1940s into the early 1950s. Rooted hair appeared in the 1950s, usually the mid-50s. The earlier wigs were made of mohair and human hair but by the 1950s dynel, saran, and nylon wigs appeared (although doll wigs can be purchased today in nearly all of these materials).

We can find beautiful plastic versions of the Kathe Kruse dolls, the Sasha dolls, and Suzanne Gibson dolls that are destined to become more valuable in future years. Suzanne Gibson's baby doll is fairly recent and was seen recently at a doll show for thirty dollars. She also sells doll house figures which she has created.

As doll collecting now holds first place in popularity, we are expecting many more pleasant surprises from doll artists and doll companies in the future. Is it any wonder doll collectors never become bored?

Vogue's "Littlest Angel" plastic doll. Mark on head: Vogue Doll 1964. Purchased at flea market, undressed and disheveled for 50 cents; value, all original, $5-$8.

R&B "Littlest Angel" hard plastic, 1956, doll. Jointed knees, rooted dark auburn hair, blue sleep eyes, molded lashes. Marks: R&B (Arranbee) on head and back. Flea market price $4.00; value $10.00.

These 3 dolls recently seen at flea market. (Left) Vinyl Indian, 1968, $3.00 price. Made in Hong Kong. (Center) "So Wee" designed by Ruth Newton, manufactured by Sun Rubber Co. All vinyl, 1957, priced $4.00. (Right) "Soupee." 12" marked Bella/Made in France on back. Original clothes, 1963, rooted blonde hair, $10. *Courtesy of Etta Russell*

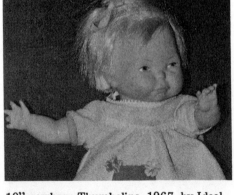

10" newborn Thumbelina, 1967, by Ideal. Vinyl arms, legs, head; rooted hair, painted features. Cloth body with pull-string that makes head rotate and body squirm. 50 cents at garage sale; all original value $5.00.

(Left) 8" Penelope by Uneeda Doll Co. Plastic and vinyl, closed eyes, 1967. 75 cents flea market, $3-$5 value. (Right) 10" Horsman "Answer Doll." All vinyl, 1966. Push button in front, head nods yes. Push button in back, head shakes no. Saved from dump.

Smallest of mass-produced SASHA baby boy as purchased in 1977 for $18.50, in own basket. Dark brown rooted hair, brown painted eyes, dark blue corduroy playsuit, white terry cloth shirt with red trim on sleeve, white leather-type shoes. Tag on arm: Sasha/Made in England.

Remco's 5½" "Heidi" and her Japanese playmate "Jan," 1966. Plastic blue container also states "Pocketbook Doll." All vinyl except plastic body. Found at garage sales for 75¢; value $5.

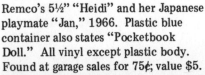

Trolls and Shanty Shack house from
the 1960s. DAM mark. Vinyl. Originals very collectible, since plastic
replicas soon followed. *Courtesy of
Anne Morgan*

Smallest of the "Miss Revlons." 10½"
Little Miss Revlon, 1957. Jointed waist,
blue sleep eyes, pierced ears, high-heel
shoes. Redressed in lovely turquoise and
silver crocheted hat and dress. Flea market
$1.50; doll book value, if all original,
$15.00.

6½" vinyl marked Furga/Italy. Stationary
eyes, blonde rooted hair. Found undressed
and messy at garage sale for 25 cents;
value, if original, $3-$4.

Kalico Kid baby by doll artist, Suzanne
Gibson. Plastic, 1977, $35.00. *Courtesy
of Fran Ellingwood, Red Barn Stage Coach
Territory, Aromas, California*

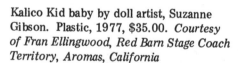

chapter 10

Doll-Like
Collectibles

Is a doll simply a toy or is it any representation of the human figure? This can be answered only in the mind of the collector. Certainly there are appealing deviations from the play doll that should be mentioned as possible collectibles. Collectors with limited display space can find small figurines very satisfying, tucked among other treasures on small shelves.

As you tread the paths to the bargain markets, you will find many figurine-type dolls that are often sold for bargain prices, although the majority of vendors tend to place a higher value on a figurine than the other glass and ceramic ware on their tables. The largest group of inexpensive figurines with a little age to them are the Japanese secondary bisques of the 1920s and 30s, still quite easy to find. They are comparable in modeling to the sugar bisque dolls of the same period. Some are simply decorative, others are bells, small vases, ring and soap holders, napkin rings, and other useful novelties.

Occupied Japan

When Japan was occupied by the Americans following World War II, export items were stamped "Made in Occupied Japan". Items with this mark are very desirable collectibles today. They were made for a short span of time during the American occupation, beginning in September of 1945 and ending in April of 1952. It is possible that no goods so marked were exported until 1948, since the Japanese ports were closed for some time after the war. There are well made pieces and others of lesser craftsmanship with the occupied marking. Some dolls are marked "Occupied Japan" as are all types of figurines, animals, banks, planters, even fish bowl or acquarium pieces. The marking is nearly always stamped on the bottom of the article, rather than being incised or identified by a sticker. At a recent local auction, figures marked "Occupied Japan" were quickly bid to an average of eight dollars each.

Advertisements and Give-Aways

During this same time, the United States was a world of give-aways and premiums, carnival prizes and bonus gifts. There were stuffed, tin, celluloid, and ceramic novelties. They are being collected, especially by those of us who nostalgically "remember when" (which isn't as far back as the Dark Ages, no matter what our children think).

It is not possible to research advertising memorabilia without finding many stories of Aunt Jemima. The original Aunt Jemima was Nancy Green, a black woman born a slave on a Kentucky plantation. In 1893, Nancy Green, as Aunt Jemima, flipped pancakes for the Davis Milling Company at the Exposition in Chicago. With her jolly disposition and her ability to captivate onlookers with song and story telling, she instantly became famous. Her beckoning, "Ise in Town Honey" was printed on hundreds of types of pancake flour advertising. Before the turn of the century Aunt Jemima rag dolls were offered as premiums, which was only the beginning of a procession of souvenirs and memorabilia that can still be collected. The Quaker Oats Company purchased the Aunt Jemima Mills Company in 1926; but by that time Nancy Green had died in a car accident. Her successor was Anna Robinson. Other Aunt Jemimas followed.

Aunt Jemima collectibles included—in addition to many rag and composition dolls—salt and pepper shakers, buttons, old advertisements and pamphlets, cookie jars, tea cosies, and syrup pitchers.

China and Bisque Figurines

Not too many doll collectors collect expensive figurines. However, we should be aware of fine figurines if only to be better able to appreciate their beauty and value.

A figurine of great artistic value must be modeled by an experienced and talented sculptor

Authentic Hummel figures. 6" with signature of Hummel on back, Goebel mark on bottom. *Courtesy of Marie Morgan*

(sculptors are often unsung heroes/heroines of outstanding doll modeling). From the Renaissance when Michelangelo (1475-1564) unlocked incomparable figures from blocks of marble, artists have expressed their feelings and those of the age in which they lived in the forms of marvelous and awe-inspiring figures. In the sixteenth and seventeenth centuries one will see the Baroque period of Europe reflected in the figurines. They showed vigorous and tumultuous movement, which were strong and brightly colored and vividly expressed.

In the eighteenth century Europe produced many of the best figure sculptors. At the famous porcelain factories in Germany, Johann Joachim Kandler (1706-1775), F.A. Bustelli (1723-1763), and J.P. Melchoir (1724-1825) were three sculptors of great repute who modeled figures of porcelain. These statuettes were designed for the banquet tables, being modeled completely in the round, so that at any perspective, the forceful and graceful figures could be enjoyed. Kandler, a court sculptor, was engaged by the Meissen porcelain factory in 1731, and from his sparkling white glazed figures came the inspiration for many other porcelain modelers. Crinoline figures of J.J. Kandler are believed to be one of his greatest contributions and several examples can be seen in the Metropolitan Museum of New York. Franc Anton Bustelli, a Swiss sculptor of great genius, modeled in the Rococo style in the eighteenth century, employing graceful, delicate design and color. J.P. Melchoir was engaged by the Hochst porcelain factory near Frankfurt as a young man and is considered one of the last of the expert porcelain modelers of that time. In

Three possible collectibles for display use. Iron stove (without lids for burners) was $1.00, small wood cradle 10¢, cup and saucer 5¢. All were found for little money at garage sales.

place of the often scrolled bases typical of Rococo. style, Melchoir sculpted grass and rock bases upon which to set his figures.

Porcelain figures have been made by Delft in Holland and France, and by English companies such as Chelsea, Derby, and Wedgwood, but Meissen porcelain of Dresden probably has been the most prolifically manufactured, especially in groups of figures. Porcelain figures are often made by molding from clay, wood, or alabaster models, which are then cut into several parts for the molds. In limited editions, Spode has produced Chelsea figures such as the Huntsman and the Fruit Seller, which are exact reproductions from the 1700s, and buyers today should expect to pay over a hundred dollars for such a figure.

In the eighteenth century, blue was the only color which could be added to the unglazed bodies and still retain color under the intense heat of the kiln. The Chinese had great success with copper reds and soon brown and many colorful glazes were produced that could stand high heat. After figures were glazed, colors and gilding were added, and the piece was placed in a lower temperature oven, called a muffle kiln. When painting in several colors, one piece could require several firings.

Royal Worcester porcelain figures created by Frederick Gertner, beginning in the early 1900s, sell for not less than three hundred dollars and many cost much, much more. Especially noted are his historical and military figures. A 1930s eight-inch Peter Pan figure designed by Gertner and produced by Royal Worcester is valued at a hundred dollars.

Freda Doughty's delicate Days of the Week and Months have also been produced by Royal Worcester, and are selling on today's market in the fifty to seventy-five dollar range. The famous Balloon Man or Woman from the Royal Doulton factory is highly prized. A 1935, 6½-inch Royal Doulton Sweeting figurine is valued near forty-five dollars, with others worth over two hundred dollars. The stoneware figurines of Jean Jacques Prolongeau, a French sculptor of impressive fame, have been chosen for production in porcelain by Haviland, and these figures are offered for approximately forty dollars. By 1960 Prolongeau had been recognized for his expert modeling.

Often pieces will be issued in "limited editions",

4" secondary china figurine, 1930s. Made in Japan. Found at flea market. *Courtesy of Lois Meade Harbert*

Collection of "Made in Occupied Japan" figures. *Courtesy of Susan Marshall*

including Christmas plates and other fine pieces of porcelain. The collector can be assured of getting a piece that will be unique, since only limited firings are made before the mold is destroyed. The price will be higher on limited editions, but they promise to escalate in value much more rapidly because of the limited manufacture.

Toby Jugs

England has been noted for its Toby Jugs since the 1700s. Wedgwood and Royal Doulton of England and Bennington of the United States are some of the famous potters who make Toby Jugs. These jugs were often modeled after Dickens' characters. They are the torsos (and also full bodies) of short stout men, always with a pouring spout, no matter how small, and were first used in Europe, made of wood or horn, as drinking tankards. Royal Doulton has also modeled Toby Jugs after famous political characters such as General Eisenhower and Sir Winston Churchill. Toby Jugs can cost from less than ten dollars for new ones to two hundred dollars or more for the older, less available ones. Some collectors deal only in Toby Jugs while other combine them with other fine pieces of porcelain and pottery.

Hummels

A group of the most appealing figurines that can still be collected today are the Hummels. Berta Hummel, an artist born in Bavaria in 1909 became, at age 25, Sister Innocentia of a Franciscan convent. The world embraced the beauty of her paintings. In 1934, exclusive rights were given to the W. Goeble Porzellanfabrik of Germany to produce bisque figures from Sister Innocentia's sketches.

It is great fun to find a Hummel or Goebel figure among the other ceramic articles on a selling table. With a quick glance at the bottom of the piece, you will see a blue pyramid-type mark (which is actually a V with a bee in the center) which will tell you immediately that this is a Goebel. You will need to look a little more carefully for the M.T. Hummel signature, since it is often incised into the figure, under the coloring of the figurines. Hummel figurines are made by Goebel. However, not all Goebel figurines are Hummel. For instance, a recent advertisement shows two small praying children 5¾ inches high created by Goebel from Charlot Byj designs, which

Aunt Jemima and Uncle Mose celluloid salt and pepper shakers. Possibly from 1930s although there was also another issue in 1950. $4 at flea market, value $8.00.

Celluloid-head Poupard doll as seen at Vallejo doll show. Poupard doll figures were used as music boxes, rattles, and elaborate novelties, most without legs and mounted on sticks. Originated in France, were very popular in 1800s. Some had fine bisque heads.

are also very adorable. There is a club which collectors can join, which brings the current prices and latest issues to its members.

In 1976, Goebel factory produced a first edition of the Christmas ornament. (These sold for eight dollars, but post-Christmas sales brought the few remaining ones down to four dollars.) Hummel and Goebel figurines are a good investment. The Hummels are not yet antiques, but have already reached great fame and have been imitated by many others. There are reproductions in figurines, needlework, calendars, pictures, and many others. A number of collectors of my acquaintance have found small pieces from the Goebel factory for fifty cents and a dollar on flea market tables, obviously overlooked by or unknown to the seller. It is great fun to pick one from a table of assorted ceramics, with the knowledge that you have at least been able to distinguish artwork from mere garbage. Sister Innocentia died in 1946, but the world shall enjoy her art for many generations to come.

Black Pottery of Mexico

In sharp, refreshing contrast to the delicately detailed china and porcelain figures are the bold black pottery forms being produced in Mexico today. Outstanding in their raw primitive beauty, they are certain to be included in many collections in the future.

San Bartolo de Coyotepec, a small village five miles south of Oaxaca, Mexico, is becoming well

A Dresden figurine of excellent modelling. Purchased in Germany in early 1950s. Comparable figurines in local shops for approximately $20 each.
Courtesy of Marie Morgan

Royal Dux figurine from Czechoslovakia with pyramid mark. Beautifully modeled porcelain. Retail price $174.95. *Courtesy of Maxine Elois, Harbour House Gifts — Monterey Wharf, Monterey, California*

known for its clay pottery and figurines. This village is like many of the small Indian villages that surround Oaxaca; in which almost all of the people in the town are skilled in a single craft. In San Bartolo de Coyotepec, the people gain their livelihood from the black pottery. A walk down the unpaved streets of the town reveals, next to the tethered goats and oxen, high piles of pottery and a pit in which the clayware is fired in every yard. These pit kilns consist of nothing more than two holes in the ground connected by a small tunnel. One of these holes has a grate near its bottom, and it is into this hole that the sculpted clay pieces are stacked. When the hole is filled with these pieces, they are covered with the remnants of broken pots until these form a cover. Then, the potter jumps into the second hole and builds a fire in the tunnel; once it is going well, he seals the tunnel at his end with clay and dirt. The fire usually burns for eight to nine hours, and after a cooling off period, the broken shards are taken off the first hole and the fired pieces removed.

Because the firing is not done at high temperatures, many of the pieces are brittle and dissolve when they come in contact with water. Usually, the pieces lower down in the hole receive a much better firing than those near the top. As a result, the clayware from San Bartolo de Coyotepec is of inconsistent quality.

The designs, however, are outstanding: beautifully sculpted peacocks and other birds; exotic mythological animals, such as lizards with five heads; and monkeys holding their tails. Many of these patterns and designs go back hundreds of years and predate the Spanish conquest of Mexico. Of special interest to the doll collector are the figur-

2¾" perfume bottles with painted wood heads for bottle caps. Probably from 1930s. Misses Rose, Gardenia, Violet, Sweet Pea, and Chypre. $9.50 (bargained down from $10.50) at antique show; seen for $5 each in collectible shops and doll shows.

nes often shaped into whistles, bells, and other dual-purpose pieces. Quite obviously molded by hand, the home craftsman adds his own personal touch to each finished model. The fine black clay needs no glazing, but is simply "polished" by rubbing the surfaces with a stone or bamboo stick. Designs are etched into or sculpted onto the clay. After drying completely, the designed pieces are put into the primitive kiln for firing.

As these doll-like figures sift into the United States, they are beginning to be found in collectible shops, garage sales and flea markets. Next time you see an example of the black pottery from San Bartolo de Coyotepec, take a few minutes to examine its dark beauty.

While the figurines from San Bartolo de Coyotepec are used as decorative household items, other dolls in Mexico are used only during fiestas and holidays. During the Feast of the Dead, celebrated on October 31 (the equivalent of our Halloween), numerous little ghoulish plaster dolls and figurines appear in the markets. These dolls are primitively made, painted white, and clothed in crepe paper. Many look like skeletons or death figures. Usually, their heads are attached to the bodies by little springs so they sway back and forth. A common motif is the bridal couple: a skeletal man and woman dressed in marriage outfits.

These figurines and dolls are displayed on the eve of the Feast of the Dead. They are usually set on a table or altar with flowers and bread and fruit; the bread and fruit are placed there for the benefit of the dead, who supposedly come to visit the family during the middle of the night.

During Christmas, a multitude of manger figures appear: the three wise men, Mary and Joseph, and the various animals. These, too, are usually placed on a family altar during the Christmas season.

Almost all major stores and markets in the large cities stock dolls and figurines from all over Mexico. There you may buy them for under a dollar. In some areas in the States they may be only slightly higher. In pottery shops or art centered areas, the price, of course, will be more. We are fortunate to be able to obtain these contemporary figures today to add to our collective treasures.

A limited edition Lladro porcelain from Spain figurine. Lladro has won prizes in Spanish National Sculpture competition in Majorca and first prize in Alvarex Dosi Foundation Competition in 1959. Use of pale pinks, greens, and grays is exceptionally effective.

Large Hummel figure. 7½", with signature of Hummel on back, Goebel mark on bottom. *Courtesy of Marie Morgan*

DOLL ACCESSORIES

Many collectors, while gathering dolls, find that there are also many accessories that may be used as accompaniments for doll displays. The most desirable doll accessories at the present time are doll houses, doll carriages, and doll cradles. Perhaps it is a desire to escape from plastic that pushes us back to the natural materials, for the beauty of wood far surpasses all others.

In the mid-1800s doll carriages often had two large iron wheels in the back for stability, with two smaller wheels in front of the cane body, giving it quite an air of elegance. In 1856, Joel Ellis, in Springfield, Vermont, began making baby carriages of maple and basswood, with wood wheels and spokes. The carriages were manufactued in two, three or four wheel designs. With leftover material, Joel Ellis fashioned doll carriages with five-inch wheels and padded seats. They were advertised as being "neatly painted and ornamented."

Doll carriages of this era also often had an attached canopy or umbrella to shade the babies. Some hooded carriages had fitted curtains tied back with dainty ribbons.

In the United States some of the first portable baby cradles were made of straw. Doll carriages in the U.S. in 1886 had the two back wheels larger than the front ones, including three-wheel carriages, which were also in vogue. Before the end of the nineteenth century, dolls in France sported wicker prams with cane wheels, their hoods daintily decorated with laces. Soon, wire spokes began to appear on carriages.

Many doll and baby carriages can still be found

Royal Doulton Toby mugs. (Left to right) 2½" Beefeater, 6½" Falstaff, 2¼" The Falconer, 3¼" John Peal, 6½" Dick Turpin. Two small mugs are 1½" and 1½".

intact kept by some loving families long after their children had children of their own. The natural-colored wicker doll buggies of the 1920s can still be found at flea markets, doll shops, and doll shows, the smallest of them usually priced at $50 or more. In 1933, Ideal Toy Company produced an all-metal-frame collapsible doll buggy with folding hood. One shop owner recently came by an old baby carriage, probably dating from near the turn of the century. Not knowing how to price it, she simply marked it $125 to see what would happen. To her amazement, the carriage was sold almost immediately. Most of the larger carriages, depending of course, upon condition and style, are selling for $100-$200, and make a beautiful addition to a doll display for the collector with available room. Several old dolls will fit comfortably into a baby carriage and make a stunning addition to a room of collectibles.

There is a new surge of popularity in doll houses. Both dolls and furniture miniatures are enjoying boom days. Some of the antique doll houses are priced very high, one recently seen was $400, while toy shops are furnishing doll houses with lighted fixtures and electronic doors.

Doll pianos were made by both Schoenut and Ellis. The Joel Ellis piano was 2 feet high and 2½ feet wide, done in rosewood finish. Albert Schoenhut, with the success of his toy piano went on to the manufacture of other toys, but it was not until four decades later that Albert Schoenhut created his famous all-wood dolls.

Some doll accessories, with a little searching, can be quite easily found today. Doll chairs and beds given up by today's children can be found at garage sales quite often for two or three dollars, but only the early bargain hunters get them, for they are snatched up quickly. If you are searching for doll beds from the early part of the century, you will need to be prepared to pay quite a high price; for instance, a mahogany doll bed from 1900 may cost a hundred dollars unless a rare bargain is found, while a 1950 canopy bed of wood may sell for around thirty dollars. Children's high chairs are great for life-size baby dolls. If you should see bargains on doll accessories, you might gather them for your next sale, for doll collectors will be grateful to find these accessories.

Porcelains by G. Pezzato, Italy. Blue sticker showing crown N. $85. *Courtesy of The Hearth Shop, Monterey, California*

3" first edition Goebel Christmas tree
ornaments, 1976. Box marked: W. Goebel,
W. Germany/sole manufacturer of the world
famous M.I. Hummel/figurines and plates.
Pink and blue, also beige. $8.00 retail.

Small figurine whistle in black pottery of
Mexico. 75 cents at flea market.

Black pottery bell figurine. Note the hand
modelling of arms and face. $1.00 in
collectible shop.

Mexican dolls commemorating Feast of the
Dead. They are dressed as Halloween
figures.

Especially nice for a doll display, this wooden piano is actually a bank, dating from the 1920s. The slot for coins is directly behind the sheet music. On the back leg of the piano is a small slip of paper stating "to remove coins pull this leg out by twisting gently." This releases the wooden peg holding a corner of the bottom undersection. 3¾" high, 5" at widest point. Piano keys are paper. 75 cents at garage sale; value $8-$10.

3¼" secondary china bell, 1930s, with bisque clapper. Marks: Made in Japan. 35 cents with chip at thrift shop; $3.00 value.

Author's doll chair from 1930s and sun bonnet blanket made by author's mother during same time. Composition doll found at flea market (badly crazed on legs) for $3.00.

Beautiful old buggy. Wicker with corduroy back, wrought iron legs. Priced $35 at outdoor antique show. *Courtesy of The Coach Shop, Santa Cruz, California*

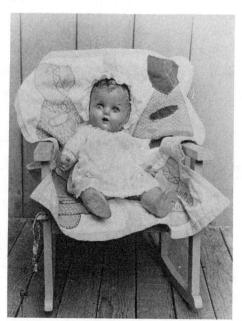

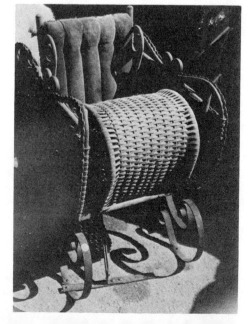

chapter 11

Doll

Investments

It is no secret that dolls are a good investment. If you shop wisely and buy shrewdly, you simply can't miss. This makes it a plausible excuse for spending all those happy but gruelling hours on the road, shopping for dolls. Doll values have gone nowhere but up over the last hundred years (or even more!) but in the last thirty years they have escalated beyond all of our dreams. Do you own a reproduction of the 1908 Sears catalogue? You will find that during that year a twenty-eight-inch Kestner doll with bisque head and kid body could be purchased for the unheard of price of $4.98. Today the same doll would no doubt sell for over $300. Or you could have mail-ordered a 45-cent bisque doll head 5¼inches in height, complete with wig, movable eyes, and two rows of teeth, ready to be sewn onto a homemade body—which would cost closer to $45 today. A Lenci doll that sold for $1.25 in 1928, now sells for over $50. A 1934 Shirley Temple composition doll complete with curls and dancing dress could be bought for $3.98; today, collectors wouldn't part with it for $100. The list is endless— even an all-cloth Little Lulu doll from the late 1950s that sold for less than $10 has a doll book price of $35.00. One flea market seller continues to bring a Little Lulu doll with him each time he sells and there it sits with a $65 price tag. This seems ridiculous, but I am keeping a close eye on him. It would not be surprising if he gets his price one day as long as he remains patient and waits for the right buyer. The

Three Tiny Tears dolls by American Character Doll Co. All have hard plastic heads. These dolls measure 11" - 15". Tiny Tears of this type manufactured to end of 1950s. Prices vary according to location. Flea markets in West $4-$12; doll shops often $25 each.

hard plastic dolls of the 1950s could be picked up at garage sales and flea markets for $1.50-$2.00 a mere five years ago. Today it is a real bargain to find one at $10, and in original condition they are worth every penny of the $20-$35 asked for the common ones.

One of the main goals of many of us who love dolls is to upgrade our collection to accumulate a valuable assemblage of the best of the dolls. This is not an easy task, especially with the prices of dolls soaring higher every year. Without unlimited funds to simply go out and purchase the dolls (if we can find them) we must therefore learn to invest carefully in dolls *of all sizes* that we can find at bargain prices; then trade or sell these dolls for ones we want to keep as part of a permanent and treasured collection.

The question the collector needs to answer, then, is what dolls can I purchase today that will increase in value at the most rapid pace?

Dolls No Longer Manufactured

As soon as the manufacture of a doll is discontinued, its value immediately increases. It doesn't have to be an old doll, as long as it is an unavailable doll. There will not be nearly enough of this particular doll to go around to each collector, so those who are fortunate enough to find one will have the advantage. Sometimes there are modern dolls that are just not popular for some reason or another. The children are not begging for them and the company stops the production. But give this doll a few years and there will be a scramble for it like the ninety-nine-cent table in the bargain basement.

Dolls that are manufactured (and hopefully marked) with company names that are no longer in business become highly prized by collectors. Many of the dolls are still available on the bargain tables. American Character Company (1918-1968) is one such manufacturer that no longer exists. Although Ideal purchased some of the molds, no more dolls marked American Character will be produced. Some of these dolls are marked "A.C.", others with the full name "American Character Doll Co." and some just "Amer Char." This company brought us the Tiny Tears dolls (see illustration). These are beauti-

Effanbee's lovely "Honey" in hard plastic, 1950. Closed mouth, brunette wig (also blondes), sleep eyes. Flea market price $10.00; doll shows and doll books $20-$30.

Two hard plastic dolls of the early 1950s. Doll on right is an Alexander doll in all hard plastic. Doll on left is "Nannette" of Arranbee (R&B) Doll Company. This type of hard plastic doll is becoming very popular in collections and has good promise for future investment. Both dolls purchased from collector for $5-$15; values $25-$50.

fully molded dolls with hard plastic heads. The first Tiny Tears has molded hair and its body was of rubber (1950). The later ones during the next five years also had the hard plastic head but inset scalp hair and vinyl bodies. All of these dolls have open mouth nursers and there is a tiny hole on each side of the upper nose for the tears. A year or so ago this doll could be found for four to six dollars—the price now generally runs ten to fourteen dollars and in certain parts of the country, especially in the East, they have also been seen for twenty-five dollars.

The Sweet Sues belonging to the American Character Doll Company are also very beautiful and becoming harder to find. They are hard plastic and have closed mouths and a rather wistful look about them—not sad and not happy. Soon you can recognize a Sweet Sue without looking for the company name on the head. Some of the Sweet Sues are as large as twenty-four inches, some have inset skull caps and others have the entire wig. Sweet Sues are still on some market tables for ten dollars (which is considered a bargain), but many sellers are becoming wise to the value of the hard plastics and raising the price to between twenty and thirty-five dollars, especially if all original and in mint condition.

Arranbee Doll Company was founded in 1922 and purchased by Vogue Doll Company in 1959. No dolls were marked Arranbee or R&B after 1961 (Vogue was purchased by Tonka in 1973). Especially outstanding for its beauty is the Nannette doll manufactured by this company. These dolls are wigged, have sleep eyes and closed mouths, and are made of a beautifully colored and buffed hard plastic. Arranbee also had a number of Littlest Angel dolls like the one illustrated. The composition Nancy reminds one of Effanbee's Patsy dolls and the composition Sonja Henie, named after the famous ice skater in the movies of the 1940s, can't be found at a doll show for less than sixty-five dollars.

Cameo Doll Company was in business by the early 1920s. Although Strombecker Corporation has purchased it, the high standards set by the original Cameo Company are still maintained. Mr. Joseph Kallus, the founder and owner of Cameo Doll Products Company worked with Rose O'Neill and her famous Kewpies, and he has retained some of the original molds of his company, now sold under the name Cameo Exclusive Products. There have been bisque, latex, stuffed, composition and vinyl Kewpies manufactured. There have been and still are imitations of Cameo's Scootles, a fat dimpled toddler with curly locks. Another of the Cameo dolls which is unusual and being snapped up by collectors is Miss Peep—the Cameo doll with the pin-hinged arms and legs (although some are not pin-hinged). This vinyl doll has stationary eyes and a lifelike baby face that makes it almost come alive. Although some of the hinged arms and legs have been broken, many dolls can still be found in very good condition. Flea market price is now nine to twelve dollars, with doll shop prices rising to thirty-five dollars.

Portrait Doll—Star Dolls and other Famous Personalities

A Shirley Temple, or a Judy Garland, or a Anne Shirley doll might not be any more beautifully modeled and gowned than a doll with an ordinary name, but that doesn't stop the price of the doll from skyrocketing with the fame of the person it represents. Perhaps we are able to relate to well-known dolls; they bring back memories of our own childhood or certain special times in our lives. The people these dolls represent are a part of our own past too.

One of the first portrait dolls to be recognized as such was the china Jenny lind doll of the 1860s. This doll has also been produced by such doll artists as Emma Clear and other doll artists. Jenny Lind was known to everyone who was fortunate enough to see her on the Barnum tours. P.T. Barnum brought Jenny Lind from Sweden to the U.S., and she sang and performed so charmingly that the American public immediately adored her. The Jenny Lind doll came onto the market, and so did other products representing her, such as beds, lamps, books, clothing, and eating dishes. This doll had black molded hair with ear puffs and a back knot. She had china arms and rosy cheeks. (The blonde singer wore a black wig on stage.)

In the 1930s when the movies and radio were our main form of entertainment, Fanny Brice as Baby Snooks came bawling and hollering over our radio tubes and gave her listeners lots of chuckles. Ideal

Two "walking" dolls. (Left) Mattel's 1964 "Baby First Step," all original, 18". Walker is molded in shoes and battery operated. Found at flea market with original box for $5; value $10-$20. (Right) Advance Doll Company's "Wanda the Walking Wonder," 1949. Metal rollers set into metal plates on shoes and wind-up key on her side; all hard plastic. At doll shows for $30-$35.

manufactured a composition Baby Snooks doll with a moldable body. Amosandra, the baby on the "Amos 'N Andy radio show" is still being found in all rubber manufactured by Sun Rubber Company. Perhaps you remember listening to "The First Nighters" on radio in the 1930s as they took us through the crowded city streets we could hear horns honking and all the noises of the city at night came into our living rooms. It was as if we were there. And at intermission they would announce "Smoking in the outer lobby or downstairs, please." Johnny of Philip Morris Tobacco Company would give his elongated chant, "Call f-o-r P-h-ill-ip M - o - r-ris". A composition and cloth body doll of Johnny was available to the public. The famous lover, Rudolph Valentino was immortalized by several companies, including the famous Italian Lenci doll. Charlie Chaplin, one of the greatest pantomime artists of all time, was created by companies over and over. At an outside antique show, one dealer had a flat metal Charlie Chaplin figure with movable hands and cap. When he moved the arms the figure tipped its hat. It was not for sale. The seller was waiting for someone to come by and exclaim that they had one—at which time he would offer to buy it. It was believed to be a carnival give-away from the 1930s.

There are too many star dolls to mention them all. Some of the better known ones from the 1930s were the composition Shirley Temple (Ideal), Jane Withers (Alexander), W.C. Fields (Effanbee), Deanna Durbin (Ideal), the Dionne Quints (Alexander), Anne Shirley (Effanbee), and Judy Garland (Ideal). The 1940s brought us composition dolls of: Scarlett O'Hara (Alexander), Margaret O'Brien (Alexander), Sonja Henie (Alexander and Arranbee), Carmen Miranda (Alexander), Rita Hayworth as Carmen (Uneeda and Alexander), and Mary Martin in hard-plastic with short lambs-wool hair, to look like her role in *South Pacific* (Alexander).

When television became a part of our lives in the 1950s, dolls were created to represent Mary Hartline of the circus; Dick Clark, host on the teen-age dance show; Dorothy Collins of *Hit Parade* in the hard plastics; Shari Lewis with her adorable puppets (Alexander-vinyl); and Baby Ricky of the Lucy and

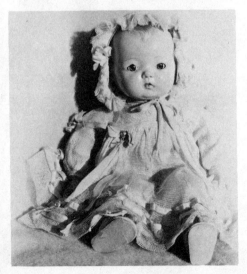

All original composition Madame Alexander doll from 1930s. Excellently modeled, molded hair, sleep eyes. Came in both blue and pink outfits of soft net with lace and ribbon trimming. Purchased from owner for $25; doll book value $75, all original.

Desi Arnaz show. Alexander produced another Sonja Henie, this time in hard plastic with a vinyl head. Anne Shirley was also produced in hard plastic, and Alexander brought us another Scarlett O'Hara, in hard plastic.

The 1960s brought us a combination of movie and television stars such as Mary Poppins (Julie Andrews) in plastic and vinyl; Julia, the nurse (Diahann Carroll) by Mattel; Buffie (Anissa Jones) and her Mrs. Beasley doll by Mattel, both stuffed and in vinyl (*Family Affair* television show); Dr. Doolittle (Rex Harrison) by Mattel in vinyl; the Flying Nun (Sally Field) in vinyl; Jeannie (Barbara Eden) from the television show *I Dream of Jeannie* in vinyl by Libby; the singing Supremes (including Dianna Ross) by Ideal in vinyl; and television's Dr. Ben Casey (Vince Edwards) in vinyl.

In the 1970s the doll business still is flourishing with such stars as Flip Wilson (and Geraldine) (as a talking stuffed doll by Shindana); Operation Boot Straps; Sonny and Cher; Donnie and Marie Osmond; the bionic man and woman; Farrah Fawcett-Majors from *Charlie's Angels* television program; Archie Bunker's grandson; and even the new Pulsar Man by Mattel whose heart beats, lungs breathe and blood flows when a button in back is pushed. As soon as a new star doll hits the market, many doll collectors immediately add it to their collection. If the past is any indication, these dolls are certain to be increasingly valuable in years to come. Watch for the unusual and the beautiful at a cheap price!

As you travel searching for dolls, you will find that you will want to keep some and release others that will not fit into your collection to other collectors.

Artists in Sculpture

The doll collecting circles are becoming increasingly aware of the many fine artists who are working in various mediums to create beautiful dolls. They are investing in these dolls as part of their permanent collections and consider them one of their dearest investments. Probably the best way to view the work of our contemporary doll artists is to attend one of the large doll conventions that are held in various parts of the United States each year. NIADA artists

Two more Alexander dolls, of more modern vintage. (Left) 13" "Sweet Tears" in original outfit, 1966. All vinyl, blonde rooted hair, open mouth nurser, black sleep eyes. $3.50 at flea market, $15 value. (Right) 11" "Kathy Cry" 1967. All vinyl, open mouth nurser, large blue sleep eyes. Marks: Alexander on head. $2 at flea market, value $12.00.

Two vinyl Shirley Temple dolls. (Left) 1958 edition, 18" all original. Pink dress, open mouth, four teeth. Tag on waist: Shirley Temple/Made by Ideal Toy Corp. *Courtesy of Lorena Lanning* (Right) 16" all original in familiar red and white polka dot dress, red shoes. Stationary brown eyes. Marked 1972/Ideal Toy Corp. Purchased for $10 in 1977.

Two well-known dolls. (Left) 14" Betsy McCall. Vinyl head, plastic body. Dark brown hair, brown eyes. By Ideal Toy Co. Marks: McCall Corporation on head, Ideal, P-90 on body. $15-$20 value. (Right) Hard plastic Sonja Henie with vinyl head, 1951. Replaced wig and dress. Slight dimples in cheek. Marked "Alexander" on head. Found for $2, value $45.

can be seen at the national convention, held in different cities, under the sponsorship of the American Federation of Doll Collectors. Artists also exhibit at regional conventions. Here you will see dolls of exquisite design that may not ever be found on any of the toy shelves or doll shops in your vicinity, since doll artists often limit their creations to a small number of dolls, and then progress on to other models. Some doll artists have contracted with doll manufacturers to use some select models, but this is the exception rather than the rule.

The National Institute of American Doll Artists (NIADA) was formed in 1963. A monograph on each NIADA doll artist is included in the two volumes of *The American Doll Artist* , by Helen Bullard, the first in 1965 and the second in 1975. Much important information on the doll artists can be gleaned from these two books. The second volume updates information on selected new artists. In 1974, NIADA was incorporated as a nonprofit organization, and foreign doll artists were asked to become associates. The products of these fine artists are treated with the respect and admiration deserving of them. New members are carefully selected and candidates for membership must meet standards stated by the NIADA code. Their dolls must have artistic intention, personalized interpretation, a high degree of craftsmanship, and the ability to convey a message through art media to the beholder.

There are many other doll artists still unrecognized. The anticipation of what the future artists will bring us is also exciting. While I was browsing through a Monterey bookstore several months ago, the young girl at the counter mentioned a friend who made dolls. I was given the name of this person to call. However, several months elapsed and it was just one of those things that didn't get done. In October of 1977, I finally contacted the young woman, Audrey (Jackie) Burnett. In the Carmel Craftmans Galley I was able to see four of Jackie's dolls. One was near the window and three others were on lighted shelves in the lovely Carmel store. These figurine dolls were exciting to see firsthand. Jackie had done three figures to represent well known women of the past from Monterey. One, Mrs. Gonzales with her child, taken from an old doctor's diary. The doctor was puzzling over why Monterey women were so healthy. From the inspiration of this diary, Mrs. Gonzales was created. (See illustration). The second doll was Rachel Larkin (Mrs. Thomas Holmes Larkin). Mrs. Larkin was one of the first European women to live in the area. The third doll near the front window was exquisitely dressed in a lavender gown and represented Eulalia Furgus, the wife of the first Spanish governor. Mrs. Furgus had come from a wealthy Spanish family and it was extremely difficult for her to adjust to the yet uncivilized Monterey area. Mrs. Furgus gave some of her beautiful clothes to Indians who she had befriended in the area, forgetting that the lavish shops where she could purchase more fashionable gowns just did not exist here! The fourth doll was done in commemoration of Pacific Grove's Feast of Lanterns celebration.

Jackie Burnett works in plastic clay for the heads of her dolls and uses expanded metal armatures. The bodies are filled out with celluclay. She models in plastic clay directly and hardens this substance in the oven. She says it takes twelve hours to model the hands, six to eight hours to model a face. It takes her approximately one week to complete a doll.

The appreciation of the modeling of dolls goes hand in hand with apprecition of all kinds of sculpture. Often the love of sculpturing is present, and an interest in dolls evolves; other times the awareness of the beauty of a doll's form brings appreciation for sculpture. It happens to doll collectors and doll artists alike.

While visiting garage sales one morning in Octo-

Kalico Kids: Toby, Amy, and Lou by Suzanne Gibson, doll artist. These plastic dolls were originally done in bisque, and the coloring is comparable to the bisque dolls. $40 each. *Courtesy of Fran Ellington, Red Barn, Aromas, California*

An unusual 20" doll by Remco in 1974.
"Mimi," the doll that sings in eight differ-
ent languages (English, French, German,
Greek, Polish, Hebrew, Spanish, and Italian).
Record battery operated. Six different out-
fits (International fashions and songs).
Mimi is now a $20-$30 value.

ber of 1977, I happened upon an unusual sculpture
that, to my untrained eye, looked very unusual and
expertly modeled. Under the figure was a slip of
paper giving some information about the artist.
Scanning it quickly (you don't hesitate too long at
garage sales) I noted that the artist, Attila von Tiva-
dor, was Hungarian-born and had come to the
United States in 1957. The more that I examined the
sculpture the more its true artistic beauty came
forth. It was very exciting. Attila von Tivadar had
first dreamed of becoming a painter, but in 1962,
with a small team of artists, he experimented with
clay and developed a process he called moreno. This
same year his art claimed great success in American
exhibitions. In 1967, he displayed his sculptures at
the Frankfurt International Exhibition, competing
with Italian, French, and Belgian exhibitors, and
won awards for outstanding quality. The next year
he studied sculpturing in Spain from the famous
Catalan sculptor, Ruigali Clovell.

Wishing to learn more about this artist, I drove
to Carmel Valley where some of his sculptures were
on display. I learned that the Attila company is
headquartered in San Francisco and that Attila often
does his sculpturing in the Santa Cruz mountains.
There were several of his sculptures in the Carmel
shop, including a sculpted head of Mecurio and
Plato, mother and child, and an interesting figure of
a football quarterback, twenty-five inches high. In
this modeling the expression of the football player is
intended to express the tremendous stress of
decision-making. It was selling for eighty-five dollars. I learned that Attila's figures are a combination
of clay, resin and wire reinforcement and are colored
to represent antique wood, although he has also
done some small figures with a white exterior.

(Left) 13½" Bionic Man (Lee Majors from television program). Marked Character/Universal City Studios, on lower back. Upper back marked 1975 General Mills Fun Group/Kenner Products. Made Hong Kong. $2 at garage sale, value $4. (Center) Mary Poppins, 1964, by Horsman. Plastic body and legs, vinyl head and arms. $2 at garage sale. (Right) 14½" plastic Lisa Littlechap, 1961. White streak in hair, eye shadow. By Remco. $1.50 at flea market, value $8-$12.

There are still bargains to find! "Scooba Doo," a 1964 doll by Mattel was found at a garage sale for 75 cents ($20 value). Original clothes, dark hair (some blonde). Pull-string talker on hips.

14" sculpture "The Beggar" by Attila von Tivadar. $69.50.

17" Eulalia Furgus by doll artist Jackie Burnett. Plastic clay head, torso, and arms. $95. *Courtesy of Jackie Burnett*

chapter 12

Gathering Items
to Sell
or Trade

The old adage, "There's more than one way to skin a cat" certainly holds true in the passionate hunt for valuable dolls. If you can't afford to buy the dolls you really yearn for, then trade, sell, bargain, create or repair—skin the cat any fun way you can devise in order to get the dolls you want. Here is where the bargain hunter can put her/his talent and time to work!

Stop and take a longer look at what might be on the bargain tables at garage sales, flea markets, and junk shops. Is there some old silver, porcelain, depression glass, or vases, or American primitives at bargain prices that could be used for trading or selling items?

This chapter is meant only to whet your appetite and give you some hints on how to obtain the dolls you really want by first purchasing other items which you can then sell or trade (at a profit, of course) to obtain the dolls you desire. You might subscribe to a collector's magazine or newspaper to find out what items are currently appealing to the myriads of people searching for memorabilia. Also, printed price guides are available at most bookstores, which will keep you in touch with today's prices. As stated before, many inside flea market sellers and some antique dealers will be cooperative in trading old items for a doll they have in their shop. When watching for bargains to trade, remember that the dealer will be reselling your trading items. Therefore, do not expect the dealer to pay you full retail price for your trade articles. In order for the shop to make a profit, you will probably be given credit for half the retail price. (In all fairness, the dealer should be giving you a good price on the doll you are trading for). Therefore buy only items you can purchase for very little cash so that your investment is kept minimal.

In this chapter, there's no place to start except at the beginning. This means that antiques are first on the agenda. For a garage sale/flea market buff, it is quite painful to educate oneself on articles over a hundred years old that one seldom sees on the selling tables. It means wading through endless material in an attempt to elicit important data on items of antiquity. It also means visiting museums, reading books, attending lectures, browsing through antique shows, and rubbing shoulders with persons much more knowledgeable in the area of antiques. There is so much material to be absorbed relating to the past arts, that it is questionable whether one ever becomes an absolute expert on anything. Only by seeing, touching and comparing antique articles, by viewing them from several angles, in different shades of light, in a quiet, peaceful atmosphere, can true acquaintance become possible. The history of the pieces soon becomes a prerequisite to understanding the full impact the modeler wished to convey. In order for us to be able to discern the good buys from the bad, and the genuine piece from the false one, we need to carry with us some knowledge of the beginnings. (For instance, once one is aware of the blue sword markings of the German Meissen factory, it is great fun to see a plate on a flea market table marked with blue swords inscribed "Made in Japan".)

PORCELAIN, EARTHENWARE AND CHINA

The earthen clay that was first modeled in its raw form by primitive Chinese cultures was often white kaolin clay, discovered by these peoples as early as the seventh century, and probably long before even that time. Although Marco Polo described the beautiful porcelain pieces he had seen in the thirteenth century, at that time only the noble and very rich were able to afford the luxury of owning pieces brought by overland routes. As ships began to visit foreign ports, all of Europe was caught in the porcelain craze.

Before all others, the Chinese potters must be commended for their beautiful artistry in the earliest porcelain pieces. From the Chinese porcelain artwork springs the inspiration for all others. In the sixteenth century, European ships sent to Asia were returning from the Chinese ports with items of such exquisite white translucency and decorated with such beautiful painting that this material known as porcelain was considered one of the most precious commodities attainable. No material was more in demand than porcelain from the Orient. Although the Chinese were perfectly willing to sell their porcelain

Meissen bowl 11" diameter. White with gold trim, hand-painted flowers. Purchased from private dealer in Germany in early 1950s. *Courtesy of Marie Morgan.*

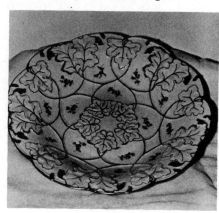

Two Meissen vases; note sword mark on bottom. Purchased from private dealer in Germany in early 1950s. Pre-World War II. *Courtesy of Marie Morgan*

Dresden hand-painted bowl. Rich yellow and flowered sections trimmed in gold. Bohler, pre-World War II. *Courtesy of Marie Morgan*

pieces to the Europeans, they were not about to tell them how they produced them. August the Strong, (1670–1733) King of Poland and Elector of Saxony, one of the most avid connoisseurs of Chinese porcelain, was determined to unearth the Oriental secrets. By 1705 August the Strong had secured the talents of an expert mathematician and physicist, E.W. von Tschirnhaus, to work on this project of developing porcelain.

During this time, a young braggart named Johann Friedrich Bottger was spreading the tale around Prussia that he could turn base metals into gold. Bottger overdid his bragging of this ability and in his rush to escape the Prussian king, who wished to have him demonstrate such talent, fled into the realm of August the Strong, where his sham was immediately discovered. However, Bottger was ordered by August to assist Tschirnhaus in his attempt to discover porcelain. Bottger and Tschirnhaus, after many experiments, had developed the basic clay by 1708, but in that year Tschirnhaus died. By 1709 Bottger had perfected both the clay and the glaze and thus it was Bottger who was given full credit for the European discovery of porcelain.

A factory was set up for Bottger in 1710 in one of August's castles (Albrechtsburg Castle) located fourteen miles northwest of Dresden. It later became the famous Meissen factory of Saxton. From that year till 1756, Meissen was the dominant factory in Europe. The secret of the composition of porcelain was kept for nine years, and great care was taken to guarantee secrecy, including the detention of workmen who were knowledgeable in the process of manufacture. But a workman from the factory escaped to Vienna and the secret was soon spread to other factories.

Old Meissen porcelain had a green hue and often collectors look for the "moons" or light spots when the piece is held up to transmitted light. The crossed swords of the Meissen Dresden factory were adapted from the Electoral Arms of Saxony in the early 1700s. There are variations of the crossed swords and these marks were pirated by many other companies. (Experience will teach you to rely on the composition of the piece itself rather than the markings.) In an attempt to discourage the copying of their porcelain, Meissen began marking their pieces after 1720, and a study of the various Meissen marks is interesting. According to some research data, the pieces of chinaware which we would call "seconds" today because of some imperfection during the manufacturing process were marked by Meissen with one or several slashes made across the Meissen swords. The more slashes, the lower its quality. Often they were sold at reduced prices or given to workmen in the factory.

For the beginning collector, identifying valuable Dresden products can be very confusing. *Anything* manufactured, or even decorated near the Dresden area can be called "Dresden". However, it should be remembered the Meissen is the pioneer and the most respected, in the judgment of the majority of experts.

Delft bulb pot. *Courtesy of Ellen Souten*

The expert will tell you that it takes practice to distinguish old porcelain from newer pieces. You will learn to recognize it in several ways—by the touch, the style, the complete appearance of the piece.

Today's porcelain pieces are, to the eye of the antique connoisseur, too perfect. Old porcelain pieces had imbedded imperfections, just as the old china doll heads often had pits and tiny bumps, authenticizing their antiquity.

Let us pause for a moment to discuss porcelain and what it really is. True porcelain is completely natural, made of two ingredients often referred to as flesh and bones. These two ingredients are 1) the white kaolin clay and 2) petuntze, a partly decomposed granite. Kaolin cannot be fused, petuntze can. Therefore, under the hot kiln temperature, petuntze fuses around the kaolin, making it one, inseparable piece. The glaze solution also becomes a part of the porcelain body under intense kiln heat. Do not expect the glaze of porcelain to be bright or glossy—its appearance will be more subdued than other chinaware. This includes bone china, which is porcelain paste with the addition of bone ash. The harder the· paste and the hotter the kiln temperature under which porcelain is fired, the more translucent it becomes.

The early Europeans (especially the English and French) manufactured what was called soft paste

Flannel from an old cigar box. Early 1900s. $1-$2 in collectible shops and flea markets, garage sales.

porcelain, which was not actually porcelain, but a mixture of pieces of glass and other components. One lecturer of antiques demonstrated to the audience that a soft paste piece has, to the flesh, a "warm" feel as opposed to the cool temperature of hard paste porcelain. (Under the rays of a short wave light, minerals in hard paste porcelain often make the piece glow, or reflect purple coloring.)

Finished porcelain, before it reaches the market, has gone through molding, firing, glazing, refiring, polishing and painting, just like the china doll heads. The variety of colors found on our patterned pieces today, is being threatened by automation. Since each color requires a separate baking, this too may fall prey to the need for moderately priced china. Also threatened with extinction are the hand painted and glazed pieces of porcelain which we still enjoy. As new methods of stenciling, silk screening, and stamping patterns on pieces of porcelain ware completely replace the older methods, even the fine porcelain pieces of this last half century may soon become unique collectibles.

There are well known manufacturers of earthenware and porcelain that had their beginnings back in the seventeenth, eighteenth, and nineteenth centuries that are still producing products of great beauty today. Because we can better relate to these pieces, a short synopsis of some of these manufacturers has been included in this chapter.

The collector should keep in mind some of the

(Left) Blue and white plate, 1920s, marked with Royal Doulton brown/ Burslem/ England. Belongs to Chisman family. (Right) Blue Ridgway plate, Chiswick, England. $4.00 at estate sale. (Center) Blue and white sugar bowl marked Blue Dresden/ 1957/Sphinx Import Co. Inc. 50 cents at flea market.

nomenclature used through the years in describing these products:

Porcelain　a shell-like, translucent, hard paste ware.

Earthenware　a non-transparent hard or soft paste ware often referred to as pottery.

Stoneware　a hard paste, glazed earthenware, used for crocks, pots, and jugs.

Salt Glaze　a transparent glaze given to some pottery while still hot from the kiln. The salt is converted into vapor before it strikes the pottery, glazing it, although pits can form in the surface from salt residues.

Slip　a mixture of a fine grade of clay and water, the consistency of cream. Can be applied to pottery as decoration or as a lining, often tinted.

Slipware　a pottery decoration used in Colonial America, composed of slips of various colors and applied to earthenware with a squeeze-type funnel comparable to our cookie decorators. Popular with Pennsylvanians.

Biscuit　unglazed pottery as it comes from the kiln.

Delft

Delftware is a tin-glazed, soft earthenware, composed of a rather coarse ground clay, with a glaze of lead mixed with ashes or oxide of tin. The surface of the old pieces was very absorbent, and the painter had to quickly brush the strokes onto the surface, giving it a bold, rather primitive appearance. By the 1600s Spain and Italy were both producing earthenware of this type, called majolica, which seems to have been named for the colorful wares produced in Italy. The English called their earthenware pieces majolica or maiolica, while the French named their product Faience after the center from which they shipped their products. Spanish and Italian wares reached the Netherlands in the 1600s and the motifs which they adapted often show the Eastern influence from porcelain of the Ming Dynasty: they colored the background white in an attempt to duplicate the porcelain, and decorated them in cobalt blue (one of the few colors that could be painted on the biscuit and fired at high temperatures in the kilns). At this time, the potters took up abandoned brewerys in the town of Delft,

Rosenthal plate found at garage sale for $1.25. Marked Rosenthal/Ivory/Phoenix/ US patent applied for. Hand painted with gold trim.

and thus the tin-glazed earthenware from this area is known as Delft.

Much of the Delft began with tiles which were blue. By the mid-1600s, with the application of two or more glazes, other colors, such as yellow, green orange, manganese purple and blue monochrome, were added to the finished piece. By 1720, enameling, the process of firing more colors over the glaze in a low temperature kiln, gave the earthenware shades of pink, gray, lilac, and opaque blue. Dutch Delft tiles were often made depicting ships, sea monsters, peddlers, farmers, musicians, and biblical subjects. Whole walls were covered with the colorful tiles (before the advent of wallpaper). The tiles were also used as a face for fireplaces.

Delftware progressed to pots, vases and tableware. Wooden platters and pewter plates were cast aside in favor of this new pottery. The Dutch displayed plates with village scenes such as windmills and water scenes. The plates were usually signed on the front, with the company name on the back.

In the early 1700s, Dutch Delftware potters migrated to Staffordshire, England. In 1665, a Dutchman from Delft, John Ariens von Hamme, had patented tile and porcelain processes as they were done in Holland. After the Delftware business appeared in Liverpool, many pieces were made for export to America (by the early 1750s). There was Delftware from the Glasgow area and many pieces were also made in Ireland. Apothecary jars and other containers (dating as far back as the 1600s) decorated with floral motifs were copied from the English silverware designs. The English Delftware does not usually have the overglaze painting used by the Dutch.

Very dramatic were the blue dash chargers—large dishes with borders of slanting blue dashes that were made to hang on walls or stand on shelves. The subjects of these charges could be anything from biblical scenes to flowers and fruit. An 1850 Delft charger of Chinoiserie design (influenced by Chinese design) would cost approximately $175 today.

Modern Delftware is hard-fire earthenware covered with slip and painted under a lead glaze. The modern Dutch Delftware can be found easily today. The local china shops carry medium to very large

Old French plate. Savequ. WS Co. 8½" diameter. *Courtesy of Marie Morgan*

plates. Available is a Dutch windmill scene marked Boch/Delfts with a sticker showing a golden crown, E & R Belgium for $18.50, or 2 portrait plates of old Dutch characters for $12.50 each.

Spode

Many fine potters came from the Staffordshire area in England. Young men were apprenticed to master potters, and this sharing of talents influenced many of the styles. Spodeware, named after Josiah Spode (1722−1797) and Josiah Spode II (1754−1827) was first manufactured in the 1770s. It is said that some of the finest blue and white Spode was manufactured from 1781−1833. Spode pioneered both stone and bone china. The beautiful English blue and white stone china intended for import to America was first produced around 1820 and the rich dark blue ware often portrayed American scenes. One of the most interesting and celebrated patterns is the tableware pattern Indian Sporting Series, created by Samuel Howitt. It includes scenes of hunters holding spears, on foot, on horseback, with hungry dogs and even riding elephants.

On the earlier pieces, some of the blues were faint, others deep. Spode is generally light in weight and the glaze is smooth and soft to the touch.

The copper plates prepared to mold Spodeware were covered with resin. With an etching needle the craftsman would draw through the copper for the pattern, opening the surface for the depth. The copper plates were dipped in acid for many bitings or immersed in acid, which would give even greater depth to the finished product. The over-glaze method was also used, with color being added after the first glazing. It was then refired at a lower temperature. Spode markings might be "Spode" or "SPODE" (these two markings are considered antique). If the word "Spode" is not marked on the plate, then it might have a circle with a cross inside. After William Copeland purchased the company in 1833, the mark became COPELAND & GARRET (to 1847) or W.T. Copeland/W.T. Copeland & Sons (at present). A Copeland dolls' cup and saucer today would sell for approximately twenty-five dollars; a cake plate from 1820 for around fifty dollars.

Small Limoge cups (name of town, not company). Gold cup on left is Rosenthal; gold and white cup on right, Furstenberg. *Courtesy of Marie Morgan*

Lenox candy dish purchased at recent garage sale for $2.00. The Lenox mark of wreath with "L."

Salt, pepper, and sugar containers, collectible today. The salt crock is stoneware from the 1920s, gift from Ruth Chisman. Sugar shaker is blue and white with "Sukker" marked Porsgrund PP on both sides of an anchor/Norway/72. $1 at flea market. Green depression glass salt and peppers in cubist pattern. Value, $15 pair.

Wedgwood

England also housed the famous Wedgwood Factory, established by Josiah Wedgwood in the 1760s, and continued by his descendants. Josiah himself had come from a family of potters. He was apprenticed to his older brother, Thomas, and was later associated with the famous potter of the 1700s, Thomas Whieldon, who also apprenticed Josiah Spode. After Josiah Wedgwood struck out on his own as a master potter, he met a Liverpool merchant, Thomas Bently, and the two men set up a pottery community named Etruria (after the Greek vases thought to be Etruscan). Wedgwood continued here until 1840, when he moved near Stoke.

The Derbyshire white clay was perfect for the famous Wedgwood cameos, and in high relief (raised parts a different color from the background) resembled ivory carvings. However, because of its extreme delicacy, perfect firing and coloring were hard to obtain with the white clay. Wedgwood sought a substitute, which he found in a fine, white artificial jasper. Thus, hard stoneware with a mat surface, Jasper, resulted in beautiful cameos in high relief, which have been and are still being imitated today. The best known Jasper is a medium blue with white relief, although there is also some done in a bluish lavender. Jasperware is known for its classical designs. There is admirable lattice work Jasper and strapwork (colored layers) which were once insets in furniture fittings in the eighteenth century. Inlaid jasperware was also used in clocks, inkstands, candlesticks, jewelry, scent bottles, fob chains, and shoe buckles. Toward the end of the 1700s, some huge Wedgwood vases with lids were made in jasperware. Smaller ones were made in the nineteenth century.

Wedgwood advertised the ability of his firm to do portraits of individuals engraved on stones for rings, lockets and bracelets. Wedgwood Basaltware, which is black stoneware named after Northern Ireland's black basaltic rocks, is also highly desirable, often seen in the more decorative tea, coffee and chocolate pots, plaques, medallions and candlesticks. The old Wedgwood pieces show the imperfections antiquers love. To them, today's Wedgwood is too white and harsh.

Creamware by Wedgwood was made throughout the nineteenth century, much of it simply decorated with a colored border edge. Wedgwood experimented to make his creamware durable and this fine ware is often passed up by unknowing collectors because of its simple and unassuming form. There was also Leeds creamware, harder and brighter than Wedgwood. Thomas Whieldon manufactured a tortoise shell creamware with a mottled brown glaze.

Wedgwood marked his products well. You may find marks such as Wedgwood / Wedgwood & Bentley / W&B / Wedgwood Etrurua / Wedgwood & Sons / Wedgwood and Co. Ltd. After 1930 Wedgwood had a chart formula for marking his pieces, and a study of these charts can reveal the month, the potter, and the year in which it was manufactured. Wedgwood has been imitated in Japan, France, and many other places, but once acquainted with the perfect work of the Wedgwood family, a collector can easily recognize the imitators. Wedgwood pieces to be found in china departments today are: a blue and white powder box for twenty-five dollars; a vase approximately four inches high for twenty-five dollars; and a small ash tray with white classical figures for ten dollars. They are incised with "Wedgwood" and the year of manufacture. There is also Wedgwood china tableware. One particularly striking pattern called Futani Crane is priced at seventy dollars for a five-piece place setting.

Belleek

Belleek is handmade tin-glazed ware and creamware that dates from 1857. Clay suitable for porcelain was found in Belleek, Ireland, in the 1850s. It is a soft paste, thin porcelain—colorless or pale cream. It is often decorated with pink, green, or yellow. Since Belleek is situated near the sea, many of the designs are nautical—mermaids, shells, and corals. On today's china shelves can be found, for instance, a lovely Belleek creamer of pale cream color with yellow handle for $16.25 or a swan approximately 4 inches high for $11.00. Belleek Christmas plates from the 1970s are still available. The 1970 Castle Caldwell, issued at $25 is now valued at over $100, although not all years will appreciate so rapid-

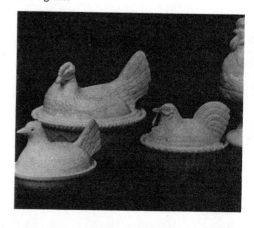

Lambs, ducks, cats, and other animals are well-liked, milk glass containers. Rooster unmarked, $3 at garage sale. (Rear, left) Westmoreland milk glass, (front, left) Westmoreland milk glass, (right) Westmoreland milk glass.

Depression glass examples. 1) Green Sunkist Reamer. $15-$20 value, seen in collectible areas for $6-$8. 2) Sugar and creamer in black cloverleaf depression glass pattern. $6.00 set. 3) Candleholder in green depression glass swirl pattern. Garage sale price $2; value $6-$10.

Iris pattern depression glass in amber. The tumblers are most difficult to find and usually cost $4-$6. Pitcher was rare find at garage sale for $1. Book value $18-$20. Sugar and creamer selling for $15, bargains $6-$8 set.

ly. However, Belleek ware is very dainty and beautiful and certainly worth discovering.

Chinaware

Lenox china is one of the most beautiful and expensive of all china dinner service available. Walter Scott Lenox, born in New Jersey, was familiar with potteries near his home and established the first Lenox factory in 1906. Lenox china is a thin, creamy, iridescent ware of exquisite beauty. A contemporary large Lenox plate, Woods Wildlife, sells for $62.50 in today's shops. A 1977 holly Christmas plate with 24-karat gold trim sells for $30. Lenox place settings generally cost today from $45-$100. All Lenox fine china patterns are hand applied and banded in 24-karat gold or platinum. Imperfect pieces never reach the consumer—they are destroyed at the factory. Some patterns available today are Fair Lady, Versailles, Flirtation, Flower Song, May Flowers, Interlude, Castle Garden, Autumn, Plum Blossons, Blue Tree and the all white with gold trim Eternal, Tuxedo and Cretan. There are also decorative pieces such as Patriots Bowl, dove dish, egg servers and a three-piece children's set. Lenox fine hand-blown lead crystal both clear and colored is also being manufactured today.

Limoges, France, has been a center for fine porcelain since 1771 and the Limoges mark is highly respected today. David Haviland, creator of Haviland china, lived in Limoges, France, in 1839. The most prized Haviland china is marked "Limoges". Since 1940 it has been made both in the United States and France.

Royal Copenhagen has been a product of Denmark since 1772. This firm is well known for its Christmas plates, which have a white background with grey or buff decoration.

The Royal Doulton Company of England is well known for its beautiful china. Royal Doulton, established in 1815, produced the onion pattern similar to Wedgwood (originally a Meissen design), and made Gibson girl plates and Toby mugs, which are still being produced. Today, Royal Doulton five-piece china dinnerware settings are averaging seventy dollars. The Tavistock pattern, for instance, with white background, trimmed with small blue, red, and yellow flowers on the rim and plate center is very striking. Minton dinnerware (manufactured by Royal Doulton) is selling for seventy dollars a place setting in a local store. Both the Grasmere pattern of blue and gold and the Avonlea pattern with blue, pink, and gold flowers set a lovely table.

There are many other fine pieces of china to be seen today. Canton, originating in China in the 1780s, is highly prized today, with typical motifs of tea houses, willows, and birds. Some of the old pieces have a clear, sharp decoration against a background of blue-gray. By becoming acquainted with what is selling today, you will be able to recognize some of the finer pieces on the selling tables tomorrow.

Stoneware

Stoneware, traditionally pottery of Germany (most famous for the beer steins and tavern tankards), is a coarse, glazed and fired pottery in the shapes of crocks, bowls, and jugs. Stoneware can be fired at a much higher temperature than earthenware and is often baked for up to three days. The colors include grays, whites, beiges, and dark browns. England was producing stoneware as early as the 1600s and Bottger, of Meissen fame, discovered a red stoneware that was even superior to the Chinese—it was so hard it could be polished on a glazier wheel. American colonists, many of German descent, brought their knowledge of stoneware with them. By 1820 they were incising patterns on the early American stoneware and decorating with a slip of cobalt blue. After the mid-century, stenciling was used. Crocks with animal, fish, flower, and butterfly designs are bringing high prices on the auction and sale tables today. The salt crock pictured in the illustration belongs to the Chisman family from the 1920-30s era, but old salt crocks were often modeled in earlier years to hang on the wall in a wooden carrier. Many of you may recall family members making sauerkraut in just such large crock pots.

GLASSWARE

Depression Glass

As Americans began to feel the impact of the Great Depression, porcelain and crystalware was beyond the budget of most persons. Thus, depression glass was born.

Collectible containers. ¼ pint and ½ pint milk bottles from Hooper Creameries of Oakland, Calif. Cobalt blue glass, with white sailboat. Value $4.50. Mason Jar marked Mason's patent Nov. 30, 1858. Value $6-$10, zinc lid. Fritola bottle for one dose lax. Cocktail shaker in heavy glass circus animal motif. Value $4-$8. Milk glass ice cream dish $1 at flea market. Morton salt cup dated 1956. Garage sale 10 cents. In front is hand painted cream pitcher, 3" height. Garage sale 25 cents.

Depression glass—that delightfully colorful and versatile glassware that brightened the drab days following the 1929 Depression (from which its name derives)—is enjoying a heyday of popularity now, more than forty years later. Some collectors may recall lifting premium pieces of depression glass from cereal boxes in the 1930s, or receiving dinnerplates as an extra bonus for attending a movie.

There are millions of pieces of depression glass still brightening the shelves of bargain shops in all areas of the United States. Patterns range from lacey motifs, fruit designs, floral etchings, thistles, cloverleafs, to tiered, swirled, blocked, bubbly or striped designs, to name a few. Most commonly, the colors are pink, green, amber, white, and crystal. Cobalt blue, and black are the most difficult colors to find. There are certain pieces of depression glass that were made in less quantity and are certainly something to watch for while browsing collectible areas. Butter dishes, candy jars, salt and pepper shakers, and candleholders, for starters, can be a great find for a collector and will command high prices. The small children's sets are ardently sought, and if one can be found in the original box, the seller can be assured of a treasure worth one hundred to two hundred dollars.

Some persons can tell whether a piece is depression glass by "tasting" it—that is, touching the tongue to the glass! Yes, there is a certain taste or sensation that some collectors swear is the way to authenticize the depression glass pieces. Whether it is the mineral content, or a combination of the components in the glass that does this, is anyone's guess, but with the modern duplication of some of the old depression glass patterns, any method to eliminate the fake from the real is worth mentioning. Other depression glass connoisseurs say that depression glass is phosphorescent under a black light. This may result from the soda ash in the sand, or—according to some—from the uranium in the sand.

Twenty-piece, four-place-setting depression glass sold originally for $1.99 in some patterns, with a service for eight costing $3.99. Shirley Temple mugs, cups, and cereal bowls were packed in General Mills cereal boxes. There were free giveaways by furniture companies and cigarette indus-

8¼" Art Deco flower frog, 1920s, in white ceramic. Marks 999. Seen at antique shops and shows for $12-$15; garage sale price $2.50. Barber bottle from 1920s, belong to author's grandmother. Red, gold-painted trim. 9". Prices for authentic old barber bottles commonly range from $45-$150.
Photo by Roger Fremier

tries. Some service stations gave away bonus pieces of depression glass. There are at least 250 known patterns of depression glass, almost all made by machine. Bubbles found imbedded in the glass are delightfully accepted as authentic flaws produced when the liquid glass flowed imperfectly into the pressing molds.

The only danger in picking up pieces of depression glass as tradables is that you may become so enchanted by this unique period glass that you won't want to part with it! There are fine illustrated books available on depression glass with guides on how to recognize this rather heavy, machine-made glass that was manufactured by such companies as Anchor Hocking, Hazel Atlas, Imperial, McKee, and Westmoreland from the 1920s to the 1940s.

There are many other collectible pieces of glassware from this era which are also being snatched up by collectors and dealers. These include the juicers or reamers which were manufactured in opaque green, blue, and ivory; and in clear pink, green, and crystal. The white Sunkist reamer is now selling for fifteen to twenty-five dollars in most western shops. The opaque green and blue reamers, some swirled and marbled with white, are very much sought. A blue reamer was seen for sale priced at forty-five dollars (some rare blues have been sold for much more) and a green at twenty-five dollars. Also keep an eye out for refrigerator dishes from the 1930s, children's divided feeding dishes, and of course the coveted Shirley Temple containers in cobalt blue, which are seldom seen for less than fifteen dollars.

Hull vases. (Left) 6" light blue and cream with rose and pale yellow tulips, lightly incised "Hull/U.S.A./108-33-6. Purchased at garage sale for 50 cents, value $12.00. (Right) Floral 8½" aqua to light pink color with rose and yellow flowers. Marks in raised letters: "Hull Art/USA-3-8½"; priced at outdoor antique show, $16.

Fostoria Glass Company

While you are searching for depression glass you will find some glassware which is daintier and often etched with simple cuttings. This will probably be Fostoria Glass. This company was founded in Fostoria, Ohio, in 1887 and in 1891 moved to Moundsville, West Virginia. In the mid 1920s 90 percent of Fostoria glass was colored, although by 1938 it had returned to the clear crystalware. All of this company's glass is handmade with simple shapes and simple cuttings and is considered to be of high quality.

Cambridge Glass Company

Cambridge Glass Company was founded in Cambridge, Ohio, in 1901 and operated until 1958. You will recognize this glassware by the trademark of a *c* in a triangle or black and gold paper label. It is opaque glassware and the most popular is the Crown Tuscan, in flesh pink. This can still be found on the flea market tables, some pieces magnificently beautiful, especially the patterned creamers and sugars, although punch bowls, vases, and many other items were also manufactured at this time.

Barber Bottles

Although my grandmother no doubt had many lovely items in her home, the only articles I can recall were two barbershop bottles she kept on a shelf in the living room. Spotting the bottles in her son's barbershop in the 1920s, she felt they were much too beautiful to throw away, and so they became a part of her home decor. They are red with gold gilding. Although these bottles are priceless to me in sentimental value, I later found that barber bottles are very rare and are admired by thousands of collectors.

Colorful bottles, set on marble-shelved barber shops were in vogue from the late 1800s into the 1930s. These many-shaped, often hand-blown bottles were often hand-painted. The best way to become acquainted with these old bottles and other types is to attend bottle shows and exhibits. The next best way is to search for books illustrating and pricing old bottles. The barber bottle you find may be worth from $50 to $150, depending upon its rarity. However, it is important to make certain the bottle is not a reproduction. Most authentic barber bottles have some residue of their original contents on the inside of the bottle. The bottom of the bottles are usually slightly scratched from being moved about on the marble barber shelves and often the color on the hand-painted bottles has dulled and chipped in some areas. You may have a reproduction if your barber bottle is too perfect, too shiny, and too clean!

Weller vase, aqua green with white wild rose. Purchased in set of three for $15. Pink satin vase with flocked flower design. *Courtesy of Ruth Chisman*

Flower Vases

Some of the most popular collectibles in American pottery are flower vases made by Roseville, Hull, and Weller companies, which are so marked on the bottom of the vases. Bargains can still be found. Sometimes lime-encrusted vases are found at garage sales or flea market tables, often for a dollar or less.

The State of Ohio seemed to be the hub of the American pottery business at the turn of the century. The Weller, Roseville and Hull pottery companies, all located there, furnished us with hundreds of exceptionally appealing vases. The Hull Pottery Company was located in Crooksville, Ohio, while Weller and Roseville factories were both located in Zanesville, Ohio. By the early 1890s these companies were producing what was termed artware. Hull pieces can be recognized by their soft flowing pastels, usually adorned with grain and flower motifs. Many of you will recall these types of vases in your home in the 1920s and 30s. By 1950 the firm was producing more utilitarian wares (including dinnerware service). Hull began their pottery in the early 1900s and fifteen years later had a fine line of art pottery. The bottom of their vases dating in the 1920s and 30s usually have the raised letters *U.S.A.*, and the words *Hull Art*, and the last line records a production number and the height of the vase. Some of the more modern Hull pieces have the words lightly incised on the bottom and covered by the pottery color. These later vases are subdued both in coloring and glaze, resembling an unglazed, satiny finish.

The Roseville Pottery Company was in business from 1898 to 1954. Many of the Roseville vases are darker in color than the Hull pottery. In the 1930s these vases were embossed *Roseville, U.S.A.* Some of their well known patterns are Monticello, Laurel, and Primrose. In 1940, they introduced the new white rose line, and an advertisement of 1941 heralds their Bushberry line. The earlier pieces have a matte glaze, but a glossy glaze was introduced toward the end. Roseville vases demand a slightly higher price than the Hull vases, depending of course upon the rarity of the patterns.

Weller Pottery began in the 1870s and produced beautiful wares until 1948. The artwares were first made in 1893. Weller pieces, especially the early ones, are much harder to find on the flea market tables, although they also are there if you do some searching. In an attempt to keep their business going

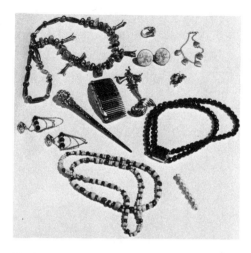

Necklaces: (Front) Red and white Hudson trade beads of American Indians. (Right) Jet black glass beads, double strand, from 1930s. (Top) Turquoise and silver necklace fashioned in Arizona. Sterling silver heart bracelet; silver ring; hand-painted earrings, porcelain-type; hatpin, comb with silver top, sterling figure pin with blue stone head, sterling earrings with gold covering, black glass and gold earrings, pearl and gold hair clasp. Purchase price from 5 cents for heart bracelet to $20-$25 necklaces.

Old cameras and pictures are sought after collectibles. (Left) Folding cartridge Kodak camera marked with patent dates. from 1908-1917. Marked EKC Kodak/ Ball Bearing shutter. (Right) This picture, Civil War era, found at garage sale for 75 cents. Leatherette case with red velvet effect on inner case.

Advertisements and printed memorabilia. (Center) Coca-cola tray is a replica taken from 1921 advertisement, garage sale 50 cents; flea markets, $3-$7. (Right) Cover of *Woman's World* magazine, Feb. 1933, framed for wall hanging. Mother and child by artist Phil Lyford. (Left) Advertisement for Pear's Soap taken from magazine of early 1900s. (Foreground) July, 1928, *Fashion Service* magazine, 1936.

during the depression, they produced beer mugs. Some of the Weller patterns worth mentioning are Louwelsea, Dogwood, Cameo, and Sicardo.

Once I found 3 Weller pottery pieces, marked $35 for the set of three (one large aqua green vase with white roses, plus two cornucopia side vases of the same pattern), only twenty minutes before the close of a show. I showed only slight hesitation in looking at the pieces, and the seller immediately offered a lower price, $22.50 for the set. I looked carefully at the pieces, mentioning my state of poverty by the end of this day, and offered (emphatically) $15 for the set. She took it.

AMERICAN PRIMITIVES

One seller asked what she called primitives, answered, "Anything from horse collars to Coca-Cola trays." In this age of plastic, Americans have become mesmerized with anything made of solid wood, including many of the kitchen items used from Colonial days till approximately the 1940s. We have a standing joke that anything with a wooden handle must now be a "primitive". One ten cent garage sale find that has a favorite spot in my kitchen is an old pump-action beater (yes, with wooden handle) and a base of circular metal rings that probably did a fairly good job of beating eggs and cream with the pushing of the handle. There are hundreds of primitive kitchen items, including potato mashers, rolling pins, pie cutters, knives, and biscuit and cookie cutters. Some early American rolling pins had iron rings at the ends; some had handsome inlays of dark wood. The Pennsylvania Dutch had folk art designs etched in the wood. During the nineteenth century there were glass, porcelain, and pottery rolling pins. There is a whole new era of kitchenware still to be collected and it is becoming hard to imagine any American kitchen, rich in the beauty of woods, not having at least one "primitive" proudly displayed on the wall. Heavy old wooden butcher tables or the bin tables with tin-lined drawers which one day held flour and sugar are other very desirable additions to an Americana kitchen. Butter churns, mayonnaise mixers, old oak ice cream buckets, even old milk crates to hold reading material, can find a place in the modern kitchen/family room area of today's homes.

ITEMS OF SILVER

It is amazing how many people will sell sterling silver jewelry at garage sales and even flea markets for a minimal price! Often they do not take the time to search for the "sterling" markings before setting them out for sale. Even more shocking is the fact that even though they may be aware it is silver, they will still sell their unwanted items for a quarter to fifty cents each. The experienced bargain hunter knows this and often takes a small magnifying glass along when searching for super-bargains. (Always get the price before getting out your tape measure or magnifying glass.) Any article marked "sterling" is valuable, be it jewelry, old hair combs with silver edges, or silver serving pieces and tableware. Nearly everyone knows that the old dresser sets in silver are extremely valuable and coveted, but watch for bargains in these too. Silver hooks to aid the lady with the high-button shoes from the early part of the century are exciting to find, and small silver boxes given as gifts from suitors are often etched with sentimental verse. Silverplate serving pieces also are popular trading items. Silverware from the first three decades of this century are climbing steadily in value. One particular silverware pattern which the author has noticed because of some early family pieces is the grape design. There are at least three patterns which carry the grape design from the 1920s and although most flea market sellers are aware of this, bargains can still be found. Single serving pieces of this silverware sell for four to six dollars, with tablespoons and larger pieces selling for as high as fifteen dollars.

OLD CAMERAS AND OLD PICTURES

Old cameras have become so collectible that clubs are being formed throughout the United States in an effort to ferret out all the old specimens before they are thrown away. Nearly every camera shop owned by independent dealers, especially, has a few old cameras tucked high on shelves or displayed in their windows. It doesn't matter that film cannot be obtained or that cases are worn and parts missing, they are part of our heritage and loved by many collectors. Another very desirable photographic item is

Advertising memorabilia. Log Cabin syrup can, bamboo and paper fan advertising soy sauce, and Faultless starch booklet, give-aways from the early 1900s. Pamphlets contain stories such as *Three Naughty Kittens, Bin & Bun, Proud Tommy Tilt.*

Cloths from "NEBO" cigarette packages, satin finish. Early part of century. Found at flea market for 50 cents each.

the old daguerreotype pictures from the civil war era. During this time they were silver-faced copper or silver plates. I found an ambrotype (image on glass) in its leatherette (black embossed cardboard) case with painted brass-colored trim for 75¢. Last Saturday at a garage sale along the oceanside a girl was apologizing for asking for a similar picture because the case had come unglued! Two years ago, pictures of this type were seen in junk shops and collectible areas for under $10. Recently they were seen in an antique show for $20-$40. Civil War pictures of soldiers can be priced as high as $150. Images of famous people can cost thousands of dollars.

PAPER COLLECTIBLES

Now, while we are in the era of great nostalgia, is the time to gather old valentines—the three dimensional love-laden cards that were decorated with cupids, lace, ribbons, snow-flake cutouts, and ornate doll-like figures. Valentine exchange began as early as the 1700s and it is quite certain that this is one tradition that will never lose its favor. Valentines from the early part of this century are still easy to find. Often the envelopes that accompany them are gracefully browning with age and only the gentlest of handling will preserve their delicate originality. People everywhere love old valentines, as well as old postcards, old hand-written cookbooks, diaries, letters, bookmarks, fans, and there are so many avid postcard collectors that they are called "deltiologists". Old magazine articles have been clipped and preserved, often framed or decoupaged to preserve their color. Sheet music from the 1920s and 30s, especially with covers featuring photographs of movie stars, are eagerly snapped up by collectors. The old breakable phonograph records can still be found also. Movie house memorabilia is being collected by nostalgic peers. Handsome movie lovers from the 1940s are still vivid memories.

ADVERTISING MEMORABILIA

Advertising memorabilia are quite obviously unique collectibles. Old campaign buttons, Coca-

Cola trays, artistic calendars by such famous artists as Norman Rockwell, and trillions of other articles link us to our past and fortunately are being lovingly collected. Old fans advertising various foods, syrup cans and jars, the Shirley Temple pitcher, cereal bowl, mug and creamer, the Aunt Jemima pitcher, President Franklin Roosevelt's Scottie, Fala, and the new 1976 Bicentennial bottles are all part of a promising treasure trove for collectors.

The Campbell Kids created in 1900 by Grace Dayton soon became famous on Campbell Soup advertisements. Campbell Kid dolls to look for include: cloth dolls, a 1948 Horsman doll in all-composition, and also a petite doll. They have been found at flea markets in vinyl by Ideal dated 1963 for four dollars a pair.

There are all types of advertising dolls to add to your selling or trading collectibles, including Ronald McDonald, Eskimo Pie Boy, Poppin' Fresh dough boy, the Jolly Green Giant, Mr. Peanuts and many others.

There are two Gerber babies, one in vinyl (1965) by Gerber Baby Food Products and another all vinyl (1971) by the same company, although the happy cherub of the Gerber baby advertisement has not been realistically duplicated, in the opinion of the manufacturer. Old magazine pictures of Gerber babies are being collected today.

Many, many areas have not been covered in this chapter. There are old clocks, inkwells, paper weights, mechanical banks, old radios and phonographs, old lamps, homemade quilts, stamps and coins, crystal and glassware, beaded purses, old bottles, and many other items. They can be researched in other books.

Once you decide to watch for collectibles, especially Americana, you will find many more keepsakes to add to your collectible trading cache. If you have the time and space to collect old furniture, there is a whole world of bin tables, wooden ice boxes, chairs, tables, player pianos, and desks that can bring a good profit to you. Educating yourself to recognize treasured old things is a continuing learning experience. It is exciting, enlightening, and joyful to make a new discovery.

Victorian mirror, metal base, bevelled mirror, circa 1880. Chisman family. Old mirrors, umbrella stands, mirror sets, carved walking canes, all of the old Americana is now much sought after.

chapter 13

Setting Up a Selling Table

The first problem that comes to mind for a collector is, how can I add old dolls to my collection if they are so rare and so expensive? There are several ways to accomplish this. Of course the easiest way to obtain old dolls is to have them handed down to you through family members or old friends. However, since few of us will be so fortunate, let us pursue other methods.

Having the money to purchase the more expensive dolls you really want is of course the main problem. There is no better way to obtain instant cash than to set up a selling table. This can be done by the following methods.

Garage Sale

A garage or patio sale is simply cleaning out all your unwanted items, pricing them, and inviting the public into your garage or patio to come and buy. By placing an advertisement in the local paper a day or two before your sale, you can be assured that the garage salers will be there when you open the doors the morning of the sale. State clearly in your ad the opening and closing time and add "no presale" to discourage over-anxious buyers from pestering you before you are set up. List a few leading items in your ad which you are certain will sell quickly. This may also catch the attention of persons who do not regularly go to garage sales; then add "plus miscellaneous" to assure the regular bargain hunters that you have much more merchandise that will also be for sale.

Some city ordinances require that the potential garage sale resident obtain a permit before being allowed to hold a garage sale. There may be limits on how many garage sales can be held at each residence per year. It is therefore wise to check with the proper authorities, usually the city manager, before holding your sale. There may or may not be a charge to obtain the permit. You will be required to list your name, address, and the dates you will be holding the sale.

As you prepare your garage for the sale, try to cover or remove from the garage all items that you are not selling. Invariably customers will be interested in those very items you had not planned to sell. If your garage is large enough to accommodate several tables on which to place your articles for sale, most of the hard work can be done the night before the sale. All of the items can be priced and placed appealingly on the tables, pictures can be hung on nails, and clothes can be placed on a clothes rack or clothesline. In the morning you will need only a few moments to set larger items such as furniture and boxes of books or records outside on the driveway area.

The selling price of the articles inside the garage should be clearly marked. Usually the greatest rush of bargain hunters will arrive the first two hours of the sale. By having everything priced, you will save yourself and the buyer a great deal of time and energy, since you will need all your wits about you during the rush hours to answer questions, bargain, and keep everything moving in a smooth manner. You may have some articles that are quite valuable, but you are not certain what price to ask. By contacting one or two antique dealers, you may obtain an appraisal of these pieces before you set them out for sale. This is also a good time to check price guide books if you have them. Always research before you sell! Then you will not rue the day you sold a beautiful old wooden bin table (as I did) for thirty-five dollars when it was worth over a hundred. Think twice before selling family treasures—your children or grandchildren may cherish them much more than a stranger would.

The more expensive collectible dolls do not sell as quickly at garage sales, since few of your customers will be doll collectors; but there will be mothers and grandmothers looking for dolls and other toys at bargain prices and you may wish to sell some of your modern dolls to make room for the better dolls you will be obtaining.

You will need to have at least ten dollars in small change ready for your customers, and a supply of dollar bills. A fishing tackle box works nicely for a cash box, since it has dividing slots for the nickels, dimes, and quarters, plus a removable tray which will hold the bills safely out of sight. It is helpful to place someone in charge of taking in all the cash and making change, usually at a table set up near the exit. Have a good supply of paper bags and boxes nearby for the buyers to tote away their purchases.

Remember that people will be looking for bargains at a garage sale. Therefore, price those articles you are anxious to clear away at a quarter or less, or even provide a free-box for customers to

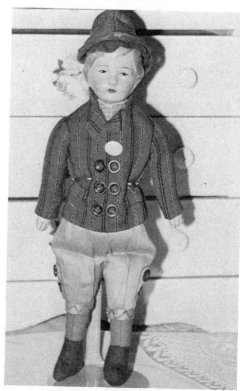

9½" Austrian composition, stuffed body, circa World War I. $22 as seen at Orinda doll show.
Courtesy of Rhoda Shoemaker

browse through. If there are certain articles you do not wish to sell unless you get full price, you might place the word "firm" under the price to discourage the bargaining customers. Do not try to sell to your customers as they enter your selling area. Garage salers like to do their own picking and choosing. What you feel is a real buy may not appeal to them and will discourage them from buying what they would be most interested in.

Flea Market

Although you will have to pack and carry all of your articles to a flea market, it is often worth the extra effort, since you will have a great many more buyers coming by your selling table. If you are planning to set up a flea market table where no reservations are available ahead of time, it is imperative that you arrive very early in the morning in order to select a good space. Corner spots are best, since you catch customers coming from both directions. By 7:30 A.M. usually all of the good spots are taken and only areas on the outlying grounds are left for the latecomers. Since you drive your car directly into the selling area of a drive-in theatre lot, the length of your vehicle reserves your space.

Certain accessories will help you a great deal in displaying your bargains. A large metal folding table is ideal for your main display in front of your car. A glass-enclosed case for your small, valuable items is very desirable. Portable display racks and clothing racks make your items not only more appealing to your customers, but the accessibility attracts buyers who otherwise would not take the time to dig through crowded boxes. Some flea market sellers have become sophisticated enough to set up shade screens over their selling area and bring with them folding chairs and small snack tables for the hours can become quite long on a selling day and the comforts of home are especially dear as the afternoon wears on. If, after bringing all the accessories possible, you are still cramped for display space, you can spread a blanket over the hood of your car and place browsing materials such as books, records, and games there.

Flea market buyers like old dishes, tools, tape recorders, almost anything that is in good condition. This is a good time to bring some of your modern dolls to sell, since you will meet more doll collectors

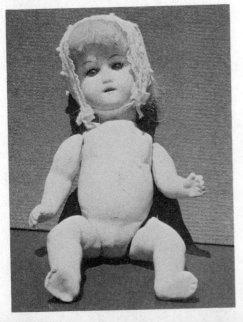

8" bisque-head doll with composition baby body. Six point star MOA marking, meaning Max Oscar Arnold. Germany, 1875-1928. Blue sleep eyes, four small teeth, socket head, blonde mohair wig. Purchased at doll show in 1977 for $45.00.

at the flea market. Mark your articles slightly higher than you would actually be willing to sell them for. This gives you room to bargain. Sometimes very curious things happen. One seller had a small silver ring marked $1.50. A dozen people tried it on, but did not buy. The seller changed the price to $2.25 and sold it to the next customer! Also changing the placing of the merchandise during the day will often help to sell those articles that are not moving. A crystal bowl, for example, could be moved to a lower level and a box of buttons moved higher. Or move the dishes from the back to the front. Sometimes it is what catches the buyers' eyes as they pass that will sell. At least try to make them curious enough to stop and look over your entire table of goods.

Although you may meet more advanced and knowledgable buyers at a flea market, they will also be willing to pay a better price to acquire the items that will fit into their collections. This doesn't mean that they will pay the price immediately, for experience brings bargaining expertise and the waiting game may last for hours, with the potential buyer passing the table several times with a slightly higher bid than the last time. As long as both parties remain good natured about bargaining, it can be great fun, and if nothing else, provides a good laugh for the day. (Check the laws for resale licenses in your area if you plan to sell often.)

7½" bisque from Germany with socket head, papier-mâché body, molded and painted shoes and stockings, dark human hair wig. Marks: R 10/0 A (Recknagel, Th.). Manufactured from latter part of 1800 to 1920s. Purchased 1977 for $30.00 ($65 value).

Doll Show

For approximately twenty to forty dollars you can reserve a booth or table at a local doll show (if it is for members only). Although the price for a table is higher, remember that *all* of the customers are interested in your merchandise. You don't necessarily have to sell dolls that are precious to you—you can bring items you have made yourself, such as apple dolls, rag dolls, doll clothes, doll houses, doll furniture, old buggies, cradles, quilts, anything pertaining to dolls for the collectors. After you have been seriously collecting dolls over a period of time, you will find that duplicates will appear in your collection . . . some that you couldn't pass up because they were such a good buy at the time. These are the dolls that should be shared with other collectors. They will bring you cash for the other dolls you will want to buy but will not take anything away from your own collection.

10" Horsman latex doll, early 1950s, stuffed body, one-piece legs and body, dimples in every joint, painted features, original dress and cap. $3 at flea market.
Courtesy of Norma Quinn

As you enter a doll show you will find pamphlets and notices of future doll shows on the first table as you enter. These will include the name and phone number of the person or persons that will be in charge of that particular show. By contacting this person, you will find out all the particulars, including time of arrival, space available, and opening and closing hours. You will need to contact this person several weeks ahead of time. By being part of the show, you will have a chance to be on the spot for the first preview. (Try to bring someone with you to help watch the table so that you can take time out to wander and gaze at all the other dolls and talk to some of the sellers during the day.) If you find a doll you are absolutely taken with, you might put a deposit to hold it until you have sold some of your dolls.

You will generally have space equal to the length of a picnic table. Bring boxes so you can "tier" the table, so all the dolls can be clearly seen. Many collectors leave modern dolls in boxes below the table for buyers to browse through, and reserve the space on the table for dolls that will bring the highest prices.

National doll shows are more expensive for the seller to enter, but also have bonus benefits. For example, you may have to pay $60 to $120 to enter a national doll show, but this may include your lodging, food, workshops, and special gifts and door prizes. Since doll collecting has become such a popular hobby, some of the larger doll shows are open to doll club members only for either all or part of the show time (which may last several days). If you do not belong to a doll club, you might check with one of your local doll club members for more information about coming shows. Reservations for doll clubs to hold their doll shows are being made two and three years ahead of time in the national organizations. If you cannot find any source of information on coming shows, a doll hospital will usually have the data available for you.

Doll shows are usually held in large hotel banquet rooms, civic halls, and large auditoriums. It is a great experience to attend your first doll show. If you are interested in the current prices of dolls, you might take along a note pad to jot down prices, since the large array of dolls is at first overwhelming. The

information can slip from your mind and you may
be able to recall only a few outstanding dolls that especially impressed you. Doll shows are great fun
and it is invigorating to be in the company of so
many fine people who share with you the wonderful hobby of doll collecting.

Selling to an Auction House

You may have some valuable doll furniture or dishes
or even dolls that you do not wish to sell yourself.
Then you might explore the possiblity of having
them sold at an auction. Generally the auction house
will claim 35 percent of the selling price. If you have
a great many items to sell or large pieces of doll
furniture, the auction house will come by your home
to pick them up. Be certain that you receive a receipt.
Your items will be tagged and inventoried as they arrive at the auction room.

Many auction houses have a preview so that
customers may come in and examine the items before they go up for bid. The items may be looked
over several days before the auction, or there may be
a preview night at the auction house. (This is a good
way to find dolls yourself.) Some auction houses offer customers an absentee bid form, which they sign
after placing a total bid on an item. If no one bids
higher than this amount during the auction, the
customer can then claim his item the next day. Often
the competition of bidding will raise the price of the
doll you are selling and will more than cover the per-
centage which the auction house will charge you. A
day or two after the auction, the auction house will
have a check ready for you for the items that were
sold.

Jody M. Doll portrait. Fine hand-
dyed muslin and kapok. Some have
complete wardrobes. Doll artist,
Jody Mehaffie. Jody sells for $65.00.
*Photo by Shipp Studio; Courtesy of
Jody Mehaffie*

Selling on Consignment

There is one last way to sell some of your dolls or
other articles. That is by placing them on consign-
ment in a doll shop or collectible store. This is the
least desirable method, since it often takes a long
time to receive the cash (you don't get paid until
someone buys the doll), and the seller gets a rather
large commission for placing your articles for sale in
the shop. However, if you do not have another doll
in mind that you are hoping to buy immediately
from the money received, patience will often pay off
in the long run by selling in this manner.

bibliography

Anderton, Johana Gast. *Twentieth Century Dolls: From Bisque to Vinyl,* rev. ed. Kansas City, Mo.: Athena, 1974.

Angione, Genevieve. *All Bisque and Half Bisque Dolls.* Nashville, Tenn.: Thomas Nelson, 1969.

Bachman, Manfred. *Dolls the Wide World Over.* New York: Crown, 1973.

Bedford, John. *Delftware.* New York: Walker and Co., 1966.

____. *Old Spode China.* New York: Walker and Co., 1969.

____. *Looking in Junk Shops.* New York: David McKay, 1961.

Bullard, Helen. *The American Doll Artist.* Vol. I, 2nd ed., Falls Church, Virginia: Summit Press, 1965. Vol. II, Kansas City, Mo.: Athena, 1975.

Cannel, Elaine. *How to Invest in Beautiful Things Without Being a Millionaire.* New York: David McKay, 1971.

Carson, Gerald. *The Old Country Store.* New York: Oxford Universtiy Press, 1954.

Christopher, Catherine. *The Complete Book of Doll Making and Collecting,* 2nd rev. ed. New York: Dover, 1971.

Coleman, Dorothy, and Evelyn Elizabeth. *The Collector's Encyclopedia of Dolls.* New York: Crown, 1968.

Eaton, Faith. *Dolls in Color.* New York: Macmillan, 1976.

Flayderman, Norman, and Edna Lagerwall. *Collecting Tomorrow's Antiques Today.* Garden City, N.Y.: Doubleday, 1972.

Fraser, Antonia. *Dolls.* London: Octopus Books, 1963.

Honey, William B. *Dresden China.* Albany, N.Y.: Fort Orange Press, 1946.

Jenkins, Dorothy. *A Fortune in the Junk Pile.* New York: Crown, 1963.

Klamkin, Marian. *Depression Glass Collector's Price Guide.* New York: Hawthorn, 1974.

Kovel, Ralph and Terry Kovel. *The Kovels' Complete Antique Price List.* New York: Crown, 1975-76.

Mebane, John. *Collecting Nostalgia.* New Rochelle, N.Y.: Arlington House, 1972.

Revi, John, ed. *Spinning Wheel's Complete Book of Dolls.* New York, Galahad Books, 1975.

St. George, Eleanor. *Dolls of Yesterday*. New York: Charles Scribner's Sons, 1948.

___. *Dolls of Three Centuries*. New York: Charles Scribner's Sons, 1951.

___. *Old Dolls*. New York: Gramercy, 1949.

Smith, Patricia. *Modern Collector's Dolls*. Vols. I, II, III. New York: Crown, 1974.

White, Gwen. *Antique Toys and Their Background*. New York: Arco, 1971.

Williams, S. B. *Antique Blue & White Spode*. London: B. T. Batsford, 1949.

Williamson, Scott G. *The American Craftsman*. New York: Crown, 1940.

Young, Helen. *The Complete Book of Doll Collecting*. New York: Putnam & Sons, 1967.

Other Publications

American Collector. 13920 McClellan Blvd., Reno, Nevada.

Arizona Highways. 2039 W. Lewis Avenue, Phoenix, Arizona.

The Doll Collector. Windy Acres Doll Hospital, Lynn, Indiana.

The Western Collector. 16835 N.E. Sandy Blvd., Portland, Oregon.